VIEWS OF ROME

VIEWS OF ROME

STEVEN BROOKE

ESSAYS BY

BONNA DAIX WESCOAT

JOHN VARRIANO

MALCOLM CAMPBELL

RIZZOLI
NEW YORK

For
Suzanne and Miles
and
in memory of
Molly and Nat

First published in the United States of America in 1995 by
RIZZOLI INTERNATIONAL PUBLICATIONS, INC.
300 Park Avenue South
New York, NY 10010

Library of Congress Cataloging-in-Publication Data

Brooke, Steven.
    Views of Rome / Steven Brooke.
        p.   cm.
    ISBN 0-8478-1881-0 (HC)
    1. Rome (Italy)—Description and travel. 2. Historic buildings—Italy—
Rome. 3. Rome (Italy)—Buildings, structures, etc. 4. Rome (Italy) in art.
5. Photography, Artistic. 6. Architecture, Roman-Italy—Rome. I. Title
DG816.B76 1995   95-999
945'.632—dc20   CIP

Printed and bound in Italy.

ACKNOWLEDGMENTS

I extend my gratitude to the officers and staff of the American Academy in Rome, in Rome and New York, for their kindness, patience, and assistance with the labyrinths of Roman life during my stay at the Academy: Adele Chatfield-Taylor, FAAR, President; Professor Joseph Conners, Director; Pina Pasquantonio, Assistant Director; Patricia Weaver, Director of Programs; Marina Lella, Administrative Assistant; Ulderico Imperatore, Director of Finance; Christina Huemer, Head Librarian; and Paolo Imperatore of the library staff. Special thanks to Ms. Huemer for sharing the bibliography of her master of arts thesis on Piranesi.

I thank the National Endowment for the Arts for providing funds to the Academy for my 1991 Rome Prize in Design Arts; and Arthur Ross for his support of the Academy and sponsorship of the 1991 Piranesi exhibition and catalog.

I am grateful to the fellows and residents of the American Academy in Rome for their help and encouragement. Particularly generous with their time and knowledge were Gregory Leftwich, Sheree Jaros, Sarah Collyer McPhee, William Valerio, Daniel Lesnick, Michael Stanton, John Petruccione, Diane Conlin, Allan Jacobs, Tod Marder, Margaret Kuntz, Rebecca Ammerman, Albert Ammerman, Darby Scott, and Lawrence Richardson, Jr. My thanks to Dr. Michael Putnam, 1990–1991 Mellon Classics Professor-in-Charge at the Academy, for his invaluable suggestions, particularly during the formative stages of this project; to Christian Zapatka, FAAR, for his assistance with the cardinal graphic standards for the book and the exhibition; to Robert Davis, FAAR, and Daryl Davis, whose warmth and perspective were welcome antidotes for my campaign mentality; to Judith DiMaio, FAAR, for sharing her knowledge and love of Rome and for leading expeditions to many remote sites; and to Michael Graves, FAAR, Jaquelin Robertson, Alex Gorlin, FAAR, and Jorge Silvetti for their support of my work.

I am also grateful to Dr. Bonna Daix Wescoat, FAAR, for her contributions to this book and the benefit of her gifted historical perspective; to Dr. John Varriano, for his friendship and inspiration thirty years ago and valued contributions to this project; to Dr. Malcolm Campbell, for his encouragement and contribution to this book; and to his graduate students for their comprehensive catalog, *Piranesi, Rome Recorded;* to Professor Sergio Lenci, distinguished architect and Professor Emeritus of the University of Rome, for his insights and accounts of the modernist architecture movement in Rome; and to Irene de Guttry, for her invaluable *Guida di Roma Moderna.*

I thank Dottoressa Marjorie Weeke of the Vatican's Pontifical Council for Social Communications for her assistance in obtaining permission to photograph the interiors of the major churches; Alessandro Califano, Ph.D., of the Commune di Roma Belle Arte for his kindness and assistance in obtaining the critical *permessi;* and the Honorable Gilbert Callaway of the American Embassy in Rome for his interest in the Academy and his support of this project.

I am indebted as well to the sympathetic homeowners and caretakers who graciously allowed me to photograph the ruins that fate had placed on their property. Often I simply had to explain my purpose, show them a copy of the *veduta* I was trying to recapture, and wait for the two most beautiful Italian words one can hear: "*come no*" or, simply, "Well, why not?" Occasionally, strenuous explanations (and pleadings) were required to convince the disbelievers that the American on the *motorino* with the large camera (and the widely-known-to-be-prohibited tripod) might be the *next* Piranesi and that it was their historic responsibility to allow him access to that monument. Access obtained, I was usually treated to coffee, a passionately delivered (and frequently accurate) architectural history, and, invariably, suggestions for the proper locations for my own images. My thanks also go to the many kind vicars and church custodians who allowed me to photograph their buildings. Special *ringraziamente* are offered to Enzo and Maria of Ristorante Sibilla in Tivoli for their gentility and hospitality.

My thanks to Mark G. Hampton, FAIA, for continuing to set the standards; to graphic designer Barry Zaid for his assistance with the design of the book; to Dr. Perri Lee Roberts, Professor of Art History, University of Miami, for her inspiring lectures and criticism; to Sandy Neville, whose understanding and management skills allowed me the freedom to concentrate on my work; to Alberto Sakai and Yo Matsuda for their dedication and craftsmanship; to James Pinckard for his computer expertise; and to Mary Ellen Anderson in Miami and Nancy Rosen in New York for their efforts to bring this work to a wider audience.

For their forthright criticisms and support I thank Wendy Watson, Curator of the Mount Holyoke Art Museum; Joseph Rosa, Director, the Ross Gallery at Columbia University; A. Raleigh Perkins, Professor of Architecture at Pratt University in Rome; Jeanne Duval, artist and McDowell Colony Fellow; Linda Robbennolt, Professor of Photography, University of Illinois; Thomas A. Spain, architectural illustrator and Professor of Architecture, University of Miami; and photographer Bob Gelberg.

I am grateful to Diane Camber, Director of the Bass Museum of Art, and the Friends of the Bass Museum for their support of the exhibition and for organizing the exhibition tour. My deepest thanks and appreciation go to Alan Z. Aiches, Chief Curator of the Bass Museum, for his dedication to the highest standards of exhibition craftsmanship. As of 1994, the work has been exhibited at the Palazzo dell'Esposizione in Rome; the American Academy in Rome; the Arthur Ross Gallery, Columbia University; the Mount Holyoke Museum of Art; the Springfield (Massachusetts) Museum of Art; and the Bass Museum of Art. It is scheduled for exhibition at the the Michael C. Carlos Museum, Emory University, Atlanta; the Graham Foundation, Chicago; the Tampa Museum of Science and Industry; the Cummer Museum, Jacksonville; and the Santa Barbara Museum of Art. For their efforts on behalf of the exhibition, I thank the Honorable Boris Biancheri, Ambassador of Italy, the Honorable Marco Rocca, Consul General of Italy in Miami, Cathy Leff, Patti Cadby Birch, Lyn Farmer, and Ecetra Ames.

I wish to thank David Morton, my editor at Rizzoli, for a belief in my work that dates back to 1982 and the revival of the Miami Beach Art Deco district and for his unflagging support of this book; and editors Elizabeth White and Cathryn Drake of Rizzoli for their assistance and patience. To writer and editor Laura Cerwinske, my colleague of over twenty years, I offer my deepest appreciation for her unselfish and objective counsel and tireless assistance with the editing.

To my wife, Suzanne Martinson, my utmost gratitude for the benefit of her unerring eye, the example of her uncompromising professional dedication, and for her understanding, patience, and love. And my best wishes to Avy and Mel, Clarence and Ada, Paul, Naomi, Tina, Miguel, Alex, Barbara, Valerie, Miranda Clare, the Bell MacDonalds, Silvia Maria, Jeannie, Kelly, the Seitzes, Myriam, and Miles.

Steven Brooke

CONTENTS

THE AUTHORITY OF ROMAN ARCHITECTURE
BONNA DAIX WESCOAT

SINCE THE TIME BEFORE MEMORY, when a she-wolf suckled Romulus and Remus in her cave on the Palatine hill, Romans have understood the power of architecture to give shape to human experience and to lay claim to cosovereignty with nature. For the ancient emperors, architecture created the framework for a unified world stretching from the Tyne to the Euphrates Rivers. To the popes of Christian Rome, architecture gave physical shape to religious values. And few in the modern era have exploited the ritual and political significance of architecture as conspicuously as Rome's neoemperor, Mussolini. As the *caput mundi* in antiquity and the Eternal City thereafter, Rome has maintained the longest and strongest claim as the center of political and religious authority of the western world.

Architecture demonstrated, and in part helped to achieve, that authority. In the sometimes overwhelming and elusive mosaic of Rome's architecture today, we confront not only the rich history of a city but the chronicle of human action, overlapping the complex relationships of place, time, and space that frame human interaction with the environment, with each other, and with the divine.

Roman architects, using a small but highly flexible set of formal elements centered on the column and arch, created guiding architectural principles that, over the course of two millennia, would be appropriated to reinforce old values and to forge new meanings in the powerfull interplay of light and shadow, of mass and volume, of brick and stone. Steven Brooke's photographs show us once more what makes Roman architecture so compelling to the eye and spirit.

THE ESSENTIAL ELEMENTS OF ROMAN ARCHITECTURE

The constants of Roman architecture are the column and the arch. As measures of space and the symbols of triumph, they forge the visual bond uniting Augustus's Forum with Piacentini's E.U.R. Of the three classical orders, Roman architects favored the Corinthian, because it was both the most ornate and afforded the greatest flexibility. Its leafy acanthus capital, presenting the same view from all sides, works for round (pp. 51, 98, 100, 115) as well as rectilinear buildings (pp. 30, 39), and for interiors as well as exteriors (p. 137). Its shafts vary from fluted marble (pp. 39, 55) to the smooth monoliths of Egyptian gray granite (p. 48) to green cipollino (p. 30), and to creamy travertine. Its entablature provides a long horizontal surface for ornament (p. 39) or great dedicatory inscriptions (pp. 30, 48). Its fancy molded base works in concert with the plinths and

podiums that lift Roman buildings above human traffic and out of human scale.

In sequence (pp. 30, 48, 123, 136) or paired (pp. 115, 138, 201), columns establish rhythm and scale; they are the element against which we read ourselves in the urban landscape. They reflect light and create shadow to give Roman facades depth and modeling—in artistic terms, chiaroscuro. In the Roman climate of scorching summers and wet winters, the colonnade is the essential element of the all-important liminal architectural space, the portico. As a temple porch (p. 48), a church narthex (pp. 123, 124), or a covered passageway (pp. 17, 218), porticoes provide shelter and connection. Inside, colonnades serve as screens to create hierarchies of space and give direction to our movement (pp. 115, 137). And it is the special mark of Roman urban genius to use the single column (and its corollary, the obelisk) as a nodel device to center space and control view (pp. 58, 59, 124, 129, 131, 139, 164, 166, 215, 217).

Behind the fancy stone colonnades lies the real powerhouse and essential component of Roman architecture—the arch. Repeated, the arch becomes an arcade; extended, it forms a vault; turned on axis, it creates a dome. Unlike the classical orders, which have to be carved in stone by skilled masons, the arch can be wrought of humble materials, mass-produced bricks, and concrete. Considerably less expensive and more versatile than cut stone masonry, brick-faced concrete set over a wooden formwork can create immense arches, vaults, and domes that have a tensile and seamless strength unmatched by stone. The brownish red earth turned colossus is the true color of Roman antiquity (pp. 31, 62, 81, 104, 105).

Above all, the arch transformed architecture from a construction emphasizing mass to one centered on space, particularly interior space. With it Roman architects created the vast interior environments of palaces, baths (pp. 27, 144), basilicas (p. 31), and pavilions (p. 62), spaces designed for people but largely transcending human scale. The great rotunda of the Pantheon, crafted entirely of brick and concrete, creates a sphere 144 feet in diameter; like the shell of an egg, it defines an internal cosmos dedicated to the planetary gods.

Like the column, the arch could be extracted from its architectural context as the icon of triumph across the Roman world (pp. 34, 46). Straddling thoroughfares and channeling action, the triumphal arch was designed not only to be seen but also experienced.

When purely utilitarian, the arch stood unadorned (pp. 57, 69, 82, 83, 101). For structural and visual emphasis, voussoirs (wedge-shaped blocks forming the surface of the arch) could be made of a different material (pp. 65–67, 159, 181, 191) or slightly cantilevered from the surface plane (pp. 61, 74, 210). At its most impressive, the arch was clad in fine material and framed with the forms of classical architecture. Engaged travertine columns set in formal hierarchy— Doric supporting Ionic supporting Corinthian—face the concrete arches of the Teatro Marcello and the Colosseum, drawing the eye upward while the cornices assert the uninterrupted horizontality of each story (pp. 43, 53). The visual power of these buildings resides in their formal purity, created and pierced by what appears to the eye as an endless repetition of geometric form. The framed, or trabeated arch, remained a leitmotif of Roman architecture through the Renaissance (pp. 122, 125, 170, 171) and after (pp. 140, 160, 205). The utilitarian aesthetic of the unadorned arch also had its proponents, especially among the rationalists (p. 222).

Roman architecture is knit by appropriation and reappropriation of a site, a building, or a motif. Piazza Navona and the Edifici dell'Esedra rise on the foundations of imperial buildings (pp. 165, 199); S. Maria degli Angeli and Castel S. Angelo are only slight alterations of the Baths of Diocletian (pp. 142, 144) and the Mausoleum of Hadrian (p. 57). Ancient columns support the portico of S. Lorenzo Fuori le Mura (p. 139); columns from Old St. Peter's adorn the facade of Fontana dell'Acqua Paola (p. 170). Our post-modern eyes look with new interest at idiosyncratic expressions of history, such as the little medieval church of S. Nicola in Carcere (p. 121), built around an antique temple, given a Romanesque tower, later modernized with a baroque facade, now surrealistically isolated in the network of Mussolini's vision. Mussolini failed to understand that Roman buildings are not meant to be experienced in isolation. They are nearly always part of a larger context, connected by streets, bridges, and stairways and visually punctuated by obelisks, columns, and fountains. The density of this urban fabric, its sudden release in piazzas, its modulation over the hills, and dispersal in the countryside demands to be experienced.

In Rome, place retains meaning. The Capitoline Hill, which served as the center of political authority in antiquity, became for Christian Rome the seat of the secular commune. Michelangelo brought the disparate buildings on the hill into coherent relationship in the Campidoglio (pp. 172, 174), which remains to this day the symbolic center of Roman civic government. Not surprisingly, early leaders of the modern republic would choose to carve the monument to Vittorio Emanuele II (p. 202) directly into the flank of this hill, while Mussolini stationed himself at its base in the Palazzo Venezia.

Of even greater iconic significance are the places sacred to Christianity, formalized by Constantine and enlarged, rebuilt, and refurbished by popes, cardinals, and architects ambitious for the architectural expression of the apostolic see of Peter to be commensurate with its spiritual authority. Connecting these spaces—visually and physically—also became a way of crafting meaning. The master plan of Sixtus V to connect the pilgrimage churches transformed the suppliant's experience of the holy shrines (pp. 124, 129, 166). Mussolini's great traffic arteries from the Tiber to the Capitoline, from the Capitoline to the Colosseum, and from the *centro* to E.U.R. and Foro Italico united imperial and modern Rome via the transforming kinetic experience of the twentieth century, the automobile.

The History of Roman Architecture in the Views of Steven Brooke: ancient rome

Rome's rise to power had much to do with its location halfway down the Italian peninsula at a defensible crossing over the Tiber river via Tiber Island (p. 64). An excellent harbor downriver at Ostia gave it access to the Mediterranean world, and the salt pans at the mouth of the Tiber provided a ready supply of one of the most important commodities in antiquity.

Romans have always taken architecture seriously. According to mythology, founder Romulus's first civic act, on 21 April 753 B.C., was to plough a great furrow, the *pomerium*, demarcating the consecrated land for the city, where he built a wall. His twin, Remus, crossed the divide and was killed for it. Archaeology confirms small, culturally diverse Iron Age communities dotting the Seven Hills of Rome and an early wall built on the edge of the Palatine near the Forum. Life under the kings succeeding Romulus was essentially pastoral; urbanization began in earnest with the arrival of the Etruscans, whose kings ruled the city from about 625 to 510 B.C. The marshy slope between the Esquiline, Palatine, and Capitoline hills was drained to create the Forum Romanum, the public marketplace and civic heart of the ancient city (pp. 28, 29). Religious and political authority centered on the Capitoline. The residential Palatine ultimately became the imperial seat, rising above the Circus Maximus, first and largest of its kind in Rome.

During the same period when Athens was throwing off the yoke of tyranny to establish democracy, Rome expelled its kings to create a republic (509 B.C.). The Temples of Saturn and of Castor and Pollux belong to the Early Republic, although their form today reflects several later restorations (pp. 33 right, 35, 36). Extensive urban development and architectural innovation belong chiefly to the expansionist drive of the third through first centuries B.C., when Rome methodically conquered and colonized the land of her neighbors and then the rest of the Mediterranean. Exposed to the nobility of Hellenistic architecture while greatly enriched by booty, leading citizens and generals added to or repaired temples, assembly halls, and basilicas in the Roman Forum (pp. 28, 29, 35). Bridges attest to Roman engineering acumen. Interest in urban planning was inherited from the Etruscans (pp. 64, 65, 67). Small temples by the Tiber reflect the roots of Roman religious architecture in Greek and Etruscan forebears (pp. 50, 51). Tombs, located by law outside the city, include the earnestly iconic pyramid Caius Cestius built in emulation of Egyptian pharaohs (p. 63). The grand rotundas of Cecilia Metella (p. 84) and Casal Rotondo (p. 86) prefigure the imperial mausolea of Augustus and Hadrian (pp. 54, 56, 126).

Fundamental political and architectural changes occurred at the turn of the millennium. Augustus, calling himself not dictator or king but "first citizen" (*princeps*), forged an empire out of the war-torn fragments of the Late Republic. He embarked on a building campaign that would make the imperial capital reflect the power of the empire. The civic, social, and religious monuments that Augustus built or refurbished during his reign from 27 B.C. to A.D. 14 were so numerous that he could claim, with some credibility, to have found Rome a city of mud and left it a city of marble.

To relieve the increasingly overcrowded Republican Forum, Augustus built an adjacent imperial forum of lavish yet orderly proportion; its framing porticoes that house ancestral statues culminate in the Temple of Mars the Avenger to form a unified expression of dynastic authority (pp. 40, 41). He developed the region of the southern Campus Martius with the Portico of Octavia (p. 69), which framed twin temples, libraries, and one of the finest collections of art assembled in antiquity. Adjacent, his Teatro Marcello (p. 53) rose three stories from the ground in a network of concrete arches, faced in travertine and framed by the classical orders. Both the arcaded design and trabeated decoration lie at the heart of Roman architecture, consummately realized in the single most compelling visual icon of Rome, the Colosseum (pp. 43–45).

Over the next three centuries, following in the tradition of Augustus, emperors established their relationship with the city through architectural donations, giving the ancient Romans (who would come to number over a million) amenities unsurpassed until the modern era. Claudius completed the Acqua Claudia and the Anio Novus aqueducts that join over the Porta Maggiore (pp. 74, 82, 83). Vespasian and his sons built the great amphitheater known as the Colosseum (significantly, over the private artificial lake of Nero's Golden House) to accommodate 50,000 spectators at the games (pp. 43–45). Domitian built a stadium now reflected in the Piazza Navona (p.164) and began the imperial forum, finished by Nerva (p. 42), next to that of Augustus. At the turn of the century, Trajan's architect, Apollodoros of Damascus, designed the largest of the new imperial forums. It was anchored by the great Column of Trajan (p. 58), as well as a public bathing complex (pp. 80, 81) whose design and scale became the model for the third-century A.D. baths of Caracalla and Diocletian (pp. 142–144). Behind the semicircular exedra of the marble forum, brick-faced concrete vaults formed tiers of shops climbing the Quirinal Hill (p. 38).

The vision of Hadrian had the greatest impact on western architecture of all the Roman emperors. He may well have designed the Temple of Venus and Rome himself (p. 37), and was known to have been responsible for the Pantheon (pp. 47–49), a vast domed rotunda entered through a traditional temple-front facade that masked the awe-evoking space within. Here, illuminated by a single disk of light from the great oculus, Hadrian held audience. Across the river he built a mausoleum (now the Castel S. Angelo) connected to the Campus Martius by a new bridge (pp. 56, 57).

The turbulent years of the third century A.D. drew imperial attention away from Rome; new building decreased dramatically until a brief but remarkable resurgence at the turn of the fourth century. Diocletian's Baths, built in A.D. 302 (pp. 142, 143), became the largest in the imperial city, despite a shrinking population. The vaulted nave supported by deep, barrel-vaulted side aisles of Maxentius's Basilica in the old Forum, completed by Constantine even as he abandoned Rome for his new capital of Constantinople, introduced new spatial concepts that would deeply influence Renaissance architects (p. 31). The ten-sided garden pavilion known as the Temple of Minerva Medica (p. 62) further explored the potential of the domed rotunda by opening the walls with archways and windows.

Just as Rome became the city of urban amenities, it also became the city of record. Triumphal arches, the Roman symbol of military victory, crowned the most important avenues. Among the best preserved are the arch built to honor Septimius Severus (p. 32, 34), and the arch decreed in honor of Constantine's victory over Maxentius, itself decorated with reliefs from earlier imperial commemorative monuments honoring Trajan, Hadrian, and Marcus Aurelius (p. 46). Narrative columns, such as that built to honor Trajan (p. 58) or Marcus Aurelius (p. 59), commanded pride of place.

The Romans blurred the boundaries between the imperial and the divine. They maintained the shrines and temples of ancient deities, and honored deceased emperors with temples built as well-calculated acts of piety to ensure succession. Nero's mother honored the deified Claudius with a large temple precinct on the Caelian (pp. 61, 60); Titus and Domitian built a temple to their father in the Roman Forum (p. 39). The colonnade immured in the facade of the Borsa was once the temple of the deified Hadrian, built by his successor Antoninus Pius (p. 55). Antoninus Pius first honored his wife Faustina and then was honored himself in one of the most beautiful temples in the Forum (p. 30).

Both residences of the well-to-do and tenement housing were built around the public monuments of the city center. Wealthy citizens built expansive suburban villa complexes outside the city. Among the finest are the mid-second-century A.D. Villa Sette Bassi on the Via Latina (p. 96) and the Villa of the Quintilii brothers on the Via Appia (p. 85). The Deus Rediculus (p. 91), Grotto of Egeria (p. 89), and Temple of Salus (p. 90), as well as the temple incorporated into the church of S. Urbano (pp. 116, 117), were on or near the estate of Herodes Atticus on the Via Appia. Later in the third century A.D. the Gordiani family built their villa, with its Pantheon-like mausoleum and octagonal halls (pp. 92, 93), on the Via Prenestina.

Of the numerous imperial residences outside the city, the most extraordinary was Hadrian's Villa at Tivoli. Located at the source of the Aniene river and Anio Vetus and Anio Novus aqueducts, Tivoli had been an important and wealthy town since the Republican period, with its grand theater temple complex dedicated to Hercules Victor (p. 101), its exquisitely placed Republican round temple (pp. 98–100), and its Augustan tower tomb (p. 97). Hadrian's secluded villa (pp. 104–111) lay some five kilometers from Tivoli, on an unprepossessing tract of land owned by his wife, Sabina. Each of the architectural complexes, some named after favorite places Hadrian had visited in Greece and Egypt, offered a different sensory experience of light, water, space, and movement: the internally colonnaded precinct with its sheet of water, called the Poecile; the pleasure canal known as the Canopus, which ended in a deep grotto dedicated to Serapis; the Small Baths, with its pure geometric volumes; the Piazza d'Oro, with the restlessly searching curves and

countercurves of its domed entrance; and the Large Baths, with its vaults held like sheets in the wind.

During Rome's ascendance, the myth and symbolism of Romulus's wall were sufficient protection for the city, which had long outgrown its Republican defenses. By the third century A.D., however, Rome was fighting for its survival. Emperor Aurelian took measures in the 270s to protect the imperial city with a wall twelve miles in circumference that traversed older monuments and suburban villas (pp. 52, 63, 72, 74) to enclose all Seven Hills and the populous areas of Trastevere and the Campus Martius (pp. 70, 73, 75). The height of the wall was raised twice in antiquity, and with the addition of later fortified gateways (p. 71), taller towers (p. 73), Renaissance bastions and gates (pp. 156, 158, 159, 161), and neoclassical gates (p. 160), the Aurelian Wall functioned as the chief defense of Rome until 1870.

CHRISTIAN ROME

Rome had lost strategic importance in the later empire, but Constantine's battle for the city at the Milvian Bridge in A.D. 312 ensured her future significance (p. 67). Confident that his conversion to Christianity had brought him victory, Constantine now gave state authority to the outlawed faith. In spite of the protests of its aristocracy, Rome became a Christian city. While allowing the senate to honor him with traditional imperial monuments (p. 46), Constantine instituted the revolutionary idea of physically mapping Christian history in Rome, designating key sites of martyrdom, burial, or miracle. These points of worship, located on the periphery of the urban center, became the object of pilgrimage, a phenomenon that would shape Rome for the next 1,500 years. Most important were the sites of Old St. Peter's and S. Paolo Fuori le Mura, marking the apostles' burial places (p. 136): S. Sebastiano, marking the cult site of the two apostles (p. 138); and S. Lorenzo (p. 139) and S. Angese, marking the graves of these martyrs. S. Croce in Gerusalemme enshrined fragments of the True Cross (p. 141); S. Maria Maggiore located a place of miraculous vision (pp. 129, 131). Constantine established S. Giovanni in Laterano to commemorate his victory and to give political authority to Christianity; it would become the cathedral church of Rome (p. 132).

Now publicly acknowledged and imperially endowed, the Christian community found monumental form in the basilica. Originally a pagan civic structure in which the emperor held audience, the basilica form not only provided the burial area and congregational space needed for Christian ritual but also expropriated the authority of the emperor for Christ as king. Plain on the outside and spacious on the inside, the design consisted of a long, timber-roofed central nave supported by colonnades and rising above side aisles to be lit by clerestory windows. A semicircular apse at the end of the hall, framed by a triumphant archway, focused the design at the eastern end, where the liturgy was performed (p. 137). The domed rotunda also found a place in early Christian architecture as the design most appropriate for enshrining objects, such as sarcophagi (S. Costanza, p. 115), or performing specific rituals, such as baptism (Baptistery of S. Giovanni in Laterano, p. 134). Ultimately, the basilica and rotunda would merge in the Renaissance design for the new St. Peter's.

By the early fifth century A.D., Rome had become a thoroughly Christian city, its pagan temples closed and its skyline transformed by new and imposing churches now built in the heart of the urban center (SS. Giovanni e Paolo, p .124). Outside the walls, the great basilica of S. Paolo, twin to Constantine's St. Peters, rose over a smaller shrine (pp. 136, 137).

Although Rome remained the spiritual center of the West, its temporal authority diminished dramatically in the millennium that followed its fall to the Goths in A.D. 476. The populated area diminished considerably. Densely populated communities on either side of Tiber Island were surrounded by the open fields and colossal ruins of the *disabitato*. In expanding the authority of the church, Romans remained faithful to the basilical design, building S. Maria in Cosmedin (p. 120), S. Giorgio in Velabro (p. 123), S. Cecilia (p. 119), and S. Maria in Domnica (p. 125), in large part with the architectural remains of ancient structures known as *spolia*.

By the turn of the first millennium, the Roman spirit had grown defensive and factionalized. The papacy attempted to dominate the Holy Roman emperors; the allied noble families vied to control strategic territory within the city. Towers built by the emerging urban nobility now established authority in the cityscape. We can imagine hundreds of structures like the Torre della Scimmia (p. 179) or the towers behind S. Martino ai Monte (p. 121). The twelfth-century Casa di Crescenzio (p. 177) also began as a tower encrusted with stolen antique architectural elements and inscriptions. Ancient monuments such as the Teatro Marcello (p. 53), the Arch of Constantine (p. 46), the Mausoleum of Augustus (p. 54), and the Tomb of Ceceila Metella (p. 84) became the fortified houses of noble families. Hadrian's tomb, already fortified in the time of Aurelian,

and ultimately linked to the Vatican by the Covered Way, became Castel S. Angelo, the papal citadel (p. 56, 57). Bridges outside the city received fortified watchtowers (p. 66).

The twelfth and early thirteenth centuries marked a golden era for medieval Rome. The papacy emerged triumphant in spiritual and temporal affairs. In populous Trastevere, S. Maria in Trastevere (p. 140) and S. Crisogono (p. 118) were built as monumental, sumptuously decorated basilicas; S. Bartolomeo (p. 122) rose on Tiber Island. S. Maria in Cosmedin (p. 120) was largely rebuilt and given a narthex, foreporch, and magnificent campanile composed of tiered arcades in the Romanesque style. SS. Giovanni e Paolo (p. 124) and S. Giorgio in Velabro (p. 123) received colonnaded narthexes. At S. Lorenzo Fuori le Mura, a new basilica was added to the sixth-century basilica of Pope Palagius (p. 139). Many churches received campaniles (pp. 118–120, 123, 124, 129, 140). In the early thirteenth century, Pope Honorius III built a family palace on the Aventine (p. 178). Respect for antiquity took on a new dimension as the popes viewed themselves as the inheritors of Constantine's empire and the Roman people explored the possibility of a republic.

This rebirth of Rome, however, was short-lived. In 1309, the seat of the papacy moved to Avignon. Rome, no longer the *caput mundi*, and without her chief patron, the church, sank into insignificance and disrepair. When Petrarch arrived in Rome in the middle of the fourteenth century, he likened the city to a dignified yet defiled matron with disheveled gray locks and torn garments, her face overcome with misery.

The Renaissance provided new opportunity. Revived interest in antiquity attracted humanists to Rome's imperial monuments. In the second half of the fifteenth century the popes returned from Avignon, and, having ceded temporal power over Europe, initiated a campaign to remake Rome great as the center of Christian spiritual authority. Building a new St. Peter's became a central concern. Over the next 150 years, old churches received new facades, including Meo del Caprina's portico for S. Pietro in Vincoli (p. 154), Andrea Sansovino's facade for S. Maria Domnica (p. 125), and Giacomo della Porta's facade for the Trinità dei Monti (p. 146). Amid the ruins of the imperial forum rose the new church of S. Maria di Loreto (p. 147).

Eager to reconstruct the urban image of Rome, Popes Julius II, Leo X, Clement VIII, and Paul III carved straight avenues (called *rettifili*) through the medieval urban fabric to connect and thereby control significant zones on both sides of the river (pp. 166, 181). Isolated buildings gave way to coherently orchestrated complexes reminiscent of imperial Rome but rarely governed by the same drive for rectilinearity. Finest was Michelangelo's 1537 design for the Capitoline Hill (called the Campidoglio), which had remained the seat of civic government since antiquity (pp. 172, 174). A broad stair-ramp, the Cordonata, drew the viewer up to the narrow end of a trapezoidal piazza framed on three sides by buildings but open on the fourth to the panorama of the city below. A slightly domed oval piazza inscribed within the trapezoid and centered on the equestrian statue of Marcus Aurelius (then thought to be Constantine) created, for Renaissance Rome, a sense of world center, an *umbilicus mundi*, just as the Forum had been for imperial Rome. With minimal modifications, Michelangelo was able to transform the Baths of Diocletian into the church of S. Maria degli Angeli (p.144).

Papal family palaces assumed dominance in the new Rome. The greatest was the Palazzo Farnese, conceived by Antonio da Sangallo the Younger in 1516 and completed by Michelangelo in 1546 (p. 180). Although the square piazza in front enhances the monumentality of the facade, it seems essentially out of place in this city, where curves and trapezoids would predominate (pp. 127, 129, 148, 165, 166).

Despite the sack of Rome in 1527, which brought the heady confidence of the High Renaissance to an abrupt halt, the church emerged from the Council of Trent with renewed vigor and new holy orders, intent on architecturally embodying the sensate experience of Christianity. The building of the Second Rome progressed rapidly over the late sixteenth and seventeenth centuries of the baroque during the Counter-Reformation. Throughout this time Rome evolved into a city of stunning vistas, splendid facades, and interconnected piazzas enlivened by the sensations of water. Chief instigator of this new Rome was Pope Sixtus V, whose ambition to connect the pilgrimage churches initiated a program of urban redesign that continued for two centuries. Ancient Roman sculpture (pp. 173, 175), and especially the several obelisks imported from Egypt in antiquity, were relocated to become a central force in the new urban landscape. Architect Carlo Maderno first helped Domenico Fontana raise the obelisk in front of St. Peter's (p. 127), then went on to place obelisks in the piazzas of S. Maria Maggiore (p. 131), S. Giovanni in Laterano (p. 134), and S. Maria del Popolo (p. 166). A column marks the center of the piazza in front of S. Maria Maggiore (p. 129). These radiant points controlled the vistas that stretched across the hills from one end of the city to the other, transforming Rome from a

collection of disconnected enclaves into a visually and physically integrated place.

Water once again flowed in nearly every piazza, carried on new and refurbished ancient aqueducts ending in fountains fashioned as triumphal arches, such as the Fontana dell'Acqua Felice (p. 171) or the Fontana dell'Acqua Paola (p. 170). Piazzas were enlivened with delightful conceits like the Sinking Ship in the Piazza di Spagna (p. 167). By mid century, the grand aquatic allegories of Piazza Navona brought a new sculptural dimension to Roman fountains (pp. 164, 165). In due course, masterfully orchestrated flights of stairs mapped the contours of the Seven Hills (pp. 131, 167, 172, 185). Piazzas themselves began to take shape, and although work often continued over the course of two centuries, as in the Piazza del Popolo, the overall result appears remarkably coherent (p. 166).

Central to the new Rome was the rebuilding of St. Peter's, which consumed the better part of two centuries and ultimately became the visual forum for the greatest Renaissance and baroque architects and their ambitious patrons (pp. 127, 128). In 1506 Julius II commissioned Bramante to take over the project that had been initiated by Nicholas V in the mid-fifteenth century and abandoned after his death. Bramante was inspired by the scale and form of Rome's ancient buildings; he aimed to build "the Pantheon upon the Basilica of Constantine." His construction of the four central piers secured the position of the dome, but little else remained fixed until Carlo Maderno barricaded the barrel-vaulted nave behind a massive facade in 1632 and Gianlorenzo Bernini gathered up the piazza in the great arms of his keyhole-shaped colonnade of 1656. Like the city of Rome itself, St. Peter's transcends its piecemeal and contradictory design by appealing directly to our sensual and emotional responses to authority and splendor.

Rome's baroque church facades claim pride of place in today's cityscape. They control dominant axes, partial views, grand spaces, and crooked cul-de-sacs. We experience Carlo Rainaldi's facade for S. Andrea della Valle directly (p. 149), but glimpse S. Antonio dei Portughesi from a tantalizingly tangential perspective (p. 153). Pietro da Cortona's facade for S. Maria delle Pace and its tiny piazza (p. 148) is highly sophisticated in its simplicity. A semicircular pavilion of paired Tuscan columns reaches into the piazza, with the countercurving upper story acting as a diaphragm, drawing air and space into the piazza and around the facade. In the more spacious landscape outside the walls, Flaminio Ponzio designed his classically balanced facade for S. Sebastiano (p. 138), while on the Caelian, his successor Giovanbattista Soria built the imposing new facade for S. Gregorio Magno (p. 150).

In the second half of the seventeenth century, Gianlorenzo Bernini's vision of baroque classicism dominated the landscape from St. Peter's across the Ponte S. Angelo to the Quirinal. His moodier rival, Francesco Borromini, monumentalized the nave of S. Giovanni in Laterano (p.133), and, in alternation with Rainaldi, worked on S. Agnese in the Piazza Navona (pp. 164, 165). The less adventuresome Rainaldi designed a circular apse for S. Maria Maggiore that reaches into the piazza (p. 131). He also built S. Agnese, and laid out the paired churches framing the entrance to the Corso (p. 166).

Palazzi lined the major avenues of Rome and framed its piazzas (pp. 182, 183, 189). The design of the Farnese was replicated in Domenico Fontana's facade for the Lateran Palace built for Pope Sixtus V in 1585–1590 (p. 134). Decisively different was Bernini's design for the palace of Cardinal Flavio Chigi, with its colossal pilasters rising from the second story (p. 182; proportions marred by the eighteenth-century remake by Nicola Salvi). As in antiquity, grand suburban villas like the Pamphilj (p.185) lay just outside the city gates, and Villa Aurelia commanded the crest of the Gianicolo (p. 184).

Although Rome was not substantially transformed in the eighteenth century, the city did gain delightful flourishes such as the Trevi Fountain and the Spanish Steps (pp. 167, 169). In emulation of St. Peter's, the pilgrimage churches of S. Giovanni in Laterano and S. Croce received new facades: Galilei's masterpiece of the stately proportioned late baroque; and Passalacqua's superb play on the transverse oval (pp. 132, 141). Fernando Fuga's design for the central facade of S. Maria Maggiore (p.129) maintained a smaller scale, connecting the block built by Ponzio a century before. Carlo Fontana added a traditional portico to S. Maria in Trastevere (p.140). Fuga also reshaped the summit of the Quirinale by designing a new facade for the Palazzo della Consulta (p. 176) and finishing the Palazzo del Quirinale, summer palace for the popes and now residence for the president of the republic (p. 175). In the piazza, the ancient horsemen were arranged around a newly erected obelisk. Another obelisk was set before the Trinità dei Monti to anchor the vista along the Via Sistina across the city to S. Maria Maggiore (p. 146). Toward the end of the century, neoclassicism gained ground. Giuseppe Valadier's severe triumphal block over the Milvian Bridge brought an overtly military bearing to the ancient theme of the triumphal arch (p. 67).

In 1823, most of the entire basilica of S. Paolo Fuori le Mura (p. 137) burned to the ground. As one of the last great papal commissions, Pope Leo XII called for its restoration, allowing what remained of the old basilica to be demolished in favor of Luigi Poletti's reinterpreted basilical design (p. 136). Vespignani designed the portico with monolithic red granite columns; Guglielmo Calderini finished the surrounding quadriporticus.

MODERN ROME

The late nineteenth and early twentieth centuries brought the unification of Italy and the secularization of Rome, now in its third incarnation as capital of the modern nation. Plans for the Third Rome began within days of royalist troops breaching the Aurelian wall near the Porta Pia on 20 September 1870. Housing for the new government was a central concern, as was the need for offices, museums, apartment blocks, department stores, and transportation facilities to meet the needs of the rapidly expanding population. New avenues, including the broad Via Nazionale, were constructed north and eastward from the central Piazza Venezia, and great embankments were built to control the ever-flooding Tiber. Competitions (concorsi) for public commissions now replaced papal patronage.

Although they continued to draw heavily on local traditions, Roman architects were not immune to the restless search for an appropriate style that characterized nineteenth-century Europe and America. Vespignani rebuilt the Porta S. Pancrazio (p. 160) and constructed the somber facade of the Campo Verano Cemetery (p. 191). Pio Piacentini's stately design for the Palazzo dell'Esposizione, with its triumphal entrance and Palladian overtones, rises from a grand flight of stairs set back from the Via Nazionale (p. 192). Gaetano Koch drew upon cinquecento motifs for his Edifici dell'Esedra (p. 199), which surmount the ancient exedra of the Baths of Diocletian to create a splendid finale to the Via Nazionale. On the other side of the river in Prati, Calderini gave the Palazzo di Giustizia a neobaroque facade (p. 194). Raffaele Ingami built S. Giocchino for the jubilee of Leo XIII in a polyglot Italian historical style (p. 195). Cesare Bazzani's Galleria Nazionale d'Arte Moderna (p. 200) and Ministero della Pubblica Instruzione (p. 204) incorporate traditional beaux-arts design principles made stylish by the addition of abundant ornamentation in the *stile floreale,* Italy's answer to art nouveau. Foreign architects also marked Rome with historicizing buildings such as George E. Street's St. Paul's (p. 190), Edwin Lutyens's neoclassical British Pavilion (later the British Academy, p. 201), and McKim, Mead, and White's palazzo-style American Academy (p. 193).

Most architects worked in the traditional Roman materials of brick, concrete, travertine, and marble, but successful experiments broadened their palette to include glass and iron: Raffaele Canevari's Ufficio Geologico, with its glassed-in central bays (p. 188), and Giulio de Angelis's La Rinascente department store, with its multi-storied arcaded display windows (p. 205).

While the city rapidly expanded toward the ancient walls, the desire to reclaim the ancient landscape, and, by association, its authority, proved irresistible. Upon his death, Victor Emmanuel II, first king of unified Italy, was honored with a monument of imperial scale set between the imperial forums and the sacred civic center, the Capitoline (p. 202).

The drive to reveal the monuments of the ancient *centro* and provide for the new civil government created an increasingly urgent need to provide housing for the displaced working class, especially following World War I. The new garden city of Aniene, designed by Gustavo Giovannoni (p. 210), and the garden suburb of Garbatella, designed by Giovannoni and Marcello Piacentini, provided one solution: vernacular architecture set in picturesque arrangements. Innocento Sabbatini's buildings for Piazza Sempione (p. 210) conjured the image of Italian town center. At Garbatella, Sabbatini's massive Albergo Suburbano of 1927 (p. 209) stands as a stripped-down urban block, and yet its curving facade, colonnaded porch, and pedimented upper story remain faithful to Roman tradition.

The Italian rationalist movement, led by Aldaberto Libera, rejected overtly historical styles and gratuitous ornament in favor of cleanly functional, technologically grounded, modern design. Post offices and train stations provided the forum for the new movement (pp. 212, 213). Even within the new aesthetic, the sense of place and history remained a chief concern.

Marcello Piacentini, the most influential architect in Rome between the wars, argued emphatically for the essentially hierarchical nature of architecture and the appropriateness of an historical, Italian context. His stripped-down classical style, which acknowledged the essential principles of earlier Roman architecture, addressed the fascist aim for historical continuity in a monumental, modern form. Because of his strong influence on group projects such as the master plan of 1931, the Città Universitaria (1932–1933), and the Esposizione Universale di Roma (E.U.R.; 1937–1943), much of the architecture of fascist-era Rome has an internal coherence and visual strength that can stand outside the rhetorical framework in which it was conceived (pp. 218–223).

But the rhetorical framework, too, is fascinating. Following his march on Rome in 1922, Benito Mussolini determined that Rome would become a "city worthy of her glory," functionally and iconographically modern but appreciative and deserving of her past. Like many forebears, Mussolini laid claim to the ancient civic center by carving two great traffic arteries through the urban fabric to connect the Piazza Venezia with the Colosseum and the Tiber River. His archaeological agenda was specific: "The millennial monuments of our history must loom gigantic in their necessary solitude." Ancient Rome was to be made over in the image of Athens. Select monuments, such as the Teatro Marcello and the church of S. Nicola in Carcere (pp. 53, 121), were disinterred from their larger urban context and the accretions of two millennia to stand marooned on parcels of land between great avenues. The Colosseum became the hub of a huge traffic circle sending motorists south to the new Esposizione Universale di Roma (E.U.R.) and north to the Foro Italico.

These two complexes are, in their own way, masterful expressions of the neoimperial idea of Rome. E.U.R. was begun in 1937 by Marcello Piacentini as the stage for the "Olympics of Civilization." Mussolini aimed to reflect the historical authority of Rome and to create a new civic center. The rectilinear, cross axial plan and trabeated facades recall Trajan's imperial forum. The Palazzo della Civiltà Italica (p. 222), designed by Giovanni Guerrini, Ernesto La Padula, and Mario Romano, rose as a modern triumphal block: six stories of undifferentiated arcades inspired by the newly excavated urban complexes at Ostia were crowned by an attic inscription reminiscent of the imperial triumphal arches of the city center. North of Prati, the Foro Italico (formerly the Foro Mussolini) recreated even more specifically the image of ancient Rome, with a stadium adorned with marble sculpture by Enrico del Debbio (p. 216). The impetus for the complex, the union of physical and intellectual education, derived from antiquity. The Carrara marble sphere set in a larger circular fountain (p. 214) introduced a third *umbilicus mundi* to complement that of the ancient Pantheon and the Renaissance Campidoglio. The obelisks of Foro Italico and E.U.R. (pp. 339, 314) at once acknowledge the iconic place of obelisks in ancient Rome and symbolically connect the Third Rome with the greatest civic plans of the baroque city.

ROME AND THE VIEWMAKER'S IMAGINATION

JOHN VARRIANO

STEVEN BROOKE'S VIEWS OF ROME WERE MADE ALMOST exactly five hundred years after the earliest realistic printed view of Rome appeared in the 1490 edition of Jacopo Filippo Foresti's *Supplementum Chronicharum*. During the intervening centuries, countless painters, printmakers, draftsmen, and, more recently, photographers have been inspired to record their own impressions of the Eternal City. The images convey almost every imaginable response to Rome's artistic and cultural heritage, but throughout the centuries, virtually all Roman *vedute*, as such views are called, have one feature in common: they are the product of an outsider's sensibility. In part, this reflects the city's special appeal to foreign visitors, which is as celebrated in literature as it is in art. Also, it is partly the consequence of the peculiar dearth of artistic talent among Rome's native population.

Before the Unification of Italy in 1870, Rome was only one of many independent city states on the Italian peninsula. Raphael, Bramante, Michelangelo, Caravaggio, Bernini, and Borromini are among the best known of the score of painters, sculptors, and architects who migrated to Rome from other Italian city states. Curiously, the city has rarely produced artists of its own but has imported the talent required for its most important commissions. Among Italian *vedutisti* whose views helped to immortalize the Eternal City, Foresti, Tempesta, Falda, Vasi, Pannini, Piranesi, and Rossini were themselves reared in other parts of the peninsula. Each experienced Rome as an outsider, presumably laden with preconceptions formed from schoolboy studies of Roman history and its monumental remains. Perhaps even stronger were the reactions of those who ventured from beyond the Alps. Certainly in literature the city has never been more compellingly evoked than in the work of temporary residents like Goethe, Chateaubriand, Byron, and Henry James. This is no less the case in the visual arts, where the sense of wonder found in the paintings of the Frenchman Claude Lorraine or today in the photographs of the American Steven Brooke is the undeniable product of powerful cultural contrasts.

European art before the nineteenth century largely held narration as its most essential purpose. The Horacian simile *ut pictura poesis*, the notion that painting should imitate poetry, guided artists throughout the Renaissance and well into the modern period. Intellectual aspiration along with the desire for social recognition induced painters to adopt this principle as a means of maintaining their superiority over the mere artisan, who also worked with his hands but exercised little imagination. But already in the late Renaissance a compromise was born between the need to create an edifying narrative art and the love of a picturesque cityscape or countryside for its own sake. From this compromise, the *veduta* grew into the recognizable independent genre that it remains today, created primarily by artists from northern Europe who came to Rome in search of some combination of classical civilization, contemporary culture, and personal freedom.

Peter Lastman, best known as Rembrandt's teacher, was one such artist. He traveled to Italy from the Netherlands in about 1603, and after a sojourn of several years returned to Amsterdam where he spent the remainder of his life painting ambitious narrative pictures with predominantly biblical themes. His *Angel Taking Leave of the Family of Tobias* is a typical work. In the foreground Tobit and Tobias kneel before the angel Raphael, who directs a mélange of traffic that includes goats, donkeys, and a camel with a parrot on its back. The town in which the scene takes place is not Tobias's Nineveh, but Rome. Lastman and his contemporaries had never been to the Holy Land, and apart from a few woodcut illustrations in Flavius Joseph's *Jewish Antiquities*, they had little idea what it actually looked like. To northerners such as Lastman Italy, with its semitropical flora, bare, stony mountains, and antique remains, reflected an image of the ancient oriental world. The Rome depicted in most of these paintings was not always classical; however, medieval and Renaissance structures appear in Lastman's *Tobias*.

Roman topography played an even more essential role in the work of a second, larger circle of Dutch artists who visited Rome in the seventeenth century. Predisposed by their Catholicism to life in the papal city, a group of artists collectively known as the Bamboccianti made the Roman townscape a regular feature of their depictions of urban street life. Precursors of nineteenth-century realists, the Bamboccianti shunned the narrative complexities that intrigued earlier northern artists, preferring instead to paint figures of the lower socioeconomic classes engaged in rather indelicate activities. Their critical fortunes have remained unrealized principally because they shunned loftier narrative subjects. Johannes Lingelbach's *Streetscene* exemplifies the Bamboccianti idiom. Half of his composition is occupied with monumental Roman structures, but he was not overly concerned with archaeological accuracy. He sets his painting in post classical Rome, looking northward from the Piazza di Spagna up to the Via del Bobuino to S. Maria del Popolo. However, he has transported one of the Dioscuri sculptures from Piazza del Quirinale and located it next to an imaginary classical portico and Romanesque campanile. Looming over the scene and bathed in the warm sunlight of early morning is the late Renaissance facade of the Trinità dei Monti, one of the few modern structures that appealed to foreign view painters. The Spanish Steps had yet to be built. When Lingelbach made his picture, around 1670, the hillside below the majestic church was, just as he shows it, steep and rutty.

No one works for a living in Bamboccianti's paintings. People loll about playing music, playing cards, or begging. The same dog always seems to be underfoot. Everyone is oblivious to the grandeur of the monuments around them. Whereas some Bamboccianti painters were fascinated by the recreational pastimes of the chronically idle, Lingelbach portrays the harsher aspects of life of the poor. Yet if any social commentary was intended in his sympathetic rendering of this gathering of lame and needy people, it was a somewhat mixed message. Whereas their deprivation might be attributed to a mismanaged and ineffective papal government—a claim frequently made in later centuries—the same church is the agency for their salvation. The man tending the soup kitchen is a monk, a wall plaque of the Madonna hangs overhead, and the elevated church of the Trinità dei Monti, so much lighter and brighter than the surrounding buildings, is the very symbol of religious aspiration. The Age of Enlightenment, which would depose faith with reason, was still a century away.

Claude Lorraine, according to a contemporary biographer, left France as a young man to become a pastry chef in Italy. Once in Rome he took up landscape painting and never returned. His numerous representations of the Roman Forum and the Campagna Romana ignore contemporary conditions and harken to a time of pastoral sentiment that has captivated poets since the time of Virgil. One common theme in ancient poetry was seeking refuge in a *locus amoenus*, or lovely place, a landscape that offered the coolness of trees beside a shady pool or brook, the sweet shelter of a mossy cave or wood where birds sang and shepherds piped. Although Renaissance poets such as Sannazaro and Tasso revived the pastoral theme, Claude was the first visual artist to depict the enchanted, carefree world of such poetry. His pictures generally are loose interpretations of real places and real monuments. His *Roman Forum* renders the site as it was in his day (ca. 1633), but he has shifted the relative positions of the Temples of the Dioscuri and the Vestal Virgins and eliminated the Arch of Titus to allow an uninterrupted vista of the Campagna Romana to unfold beyond the Colosseum.

The human figure is always present in Claude's paintings, but its role is of secondary importance, both formally and iconographically. Unlike his contemporary Nicolas Poussin, who expressed in each of his landscapes the exact sentiment of the narrative, Claude was relatively indifferent to the demands of narrative. Whether the figures are Echo and Narcissus, Apollo and the Muses, or the Holy Family on the Flight into Egypt, the treatment of the landscape remains fundamentally the same. Like many of his early pictures, the *Roman Forum* has no specified subject matter, and the figures are only types. Herdsmen, a few Grand Tourists, and an artist are stock characters. Regardless of who they are, they occupy a lower plane than the classical monuments that rise majestically behind them. Moreover, the brighter light that falls on the architecture and the open landscape leaves no doubt as to the reverence with which Claude held these elements.

Claude's evocations of the loveliness of the Roman countryside with its picturesque ruins and contented *contadini* influenced scores of painters—Italian, French, Dutch, English, and American alike. But the impact of Claude's unique vision of Rome and the *campagna* was not felt by painters alone. His works so affected the vision of those who came to Rome for other purposes that it is not unusual to find accounts of life imitating Claude's art. Consider, for example, Chateaubriand's description in his *Recollections* of 1815 of the atmosphere in the Campagna Romana:

> A singular tint and most peculiar harmony unite the earth, the sky, andthe waters. All the surfaces unite at their extremities by means of an insensible gradation of colors, and without the possibility of ascertaining the point at which it ends, or another begins. You have doubtless admired this sort of light in Claude Lorraine's landscapes. It appears ideal and still more beautiful than nature; but it is the light of Rome.

Claude's effect on the sensibility of Roman sightseers was perhaps second only to Piranesi's. Giovanni Battista Piranesi was born in Venice in 1720, thirty-eight years after Claude's death. Although trained as an architect, he has always been more highly regarded as a printmaker, and his views of the antiquities and modern monuments of his adopted city of Rome have imprinted themselves upon the imagination of Romans and Grand Tourists alike. Piranesi did not seek the serenity of Claude's Rome. He was more impressed with the grandeur of ancient monuments than with their bucolic settings. He loved to project buildings in forceful diagonal perspectives and bathe them in direct, contrasting light. His Rome is not an eternal city; the antiquities, though still grand, are slowly being destroyed by the vicissitudes of time.

Piranesi's prints frequently play upon the contrast between the grandeur of the past and the banality or degradation of current conditions. Weeds grow rampant among the ruins while the ground level has slowly risen, threatening to engulf the finely chiseled stones and return them to their natural state. In the foreground of his *Piazza di S. Pietro*, he includes among an unsavory crowd a man urinating against an imaginary fountain. Indeed in his later prints of the 1760s and 1770s, Piranesi's beggars and vagrants are so ubiquitous and so destitute as to suggest that the noble race of Romans has decayed as utterly as their monumental architecture.

Some eighteenth-century minds viewed the demise of classical civilization in an emblematic way, seeing the broken columns and collapsed vaults as memento mori or *vanitas* symbols. John Dyer's poem *The Ruins of Rome* (1740), roughly contemporary with Piranesi's *Antichità Romae*, is typical of the genre. Gazing upon the Forum, Dyer writes,

> Fall'n, Fall'n, a silent Heap; her Heroes all
> Sunk in their Urns; behold the Pride of Pomp,
> The Throne of Nations fall'n; obscur'd in dust.

Meditations on Roman ruins were nothing new, of course. Even in antiquity, Horace composed an ode on the topic, and Renaissance authors from Petrarch to Edmund Spenser lamented the city's decline and decay. But the genre reached a natural peak during the Romantic era, spurred no doubt by the erosion of religious belief and the growing interest in more metaphysical questions of existence and the destiny of the human soul. The culmination in literature came in Canto IV of Byron's *Childe Harold's Pilgrimage* of 1818:

> Italia! Italia! thou who hast
> The fatal gift of beauty, which became
> A funeral dower of present woes and past
> On thy sweet brow is sorrow plough'd by shame,
> And the annals graved in characters of flame.

As the nineteenth century progressed, there was a notable lapse in the historical imagination of most artists who recorded their impressions of Rome. The reaction of many Anglo-Saxon visitors was tinged by religious prejudice. Some of those with Puritan backgrounds found their moral principles in conflict with the sensuous beauty they saw everywhere they looked. Since the Pope remained Rome's temporal as well as spiritual leader until the Unification of Italy in 1870, discon-

tent with the municipal government went hand in hand with reproachful jabs at what were called the "superstitions" of Catholic religious practice. Although many Protestants were content to lose themselves in archaeological study, others chose to harp on the disgraces that papal rule had imposed on the city since the Reformation. The despoliation of ancient monuments was among them, and a few early guidebooks delight in enumerating the city's many papal projects that were built of spoils from the Colosseum alone. The sight of repugnant beggars in dirty streets impressed visitors as well.

Whereas some mid-nineteenth century artists reveled in their colorful depictions of the current conditions of the principal Roman sites, another group of *vedutisti* took a rather different tack. Employing the new medium of photography, first introduced in Italy about 1840, pioneering foreigners such as Alexander John Ellis, the Reverend Calvert Jones, and Robert MacPherson objectified Roman topography in a way that had never been done before. The new technology followed the older practice of using a camera obscura for perspective compositions, but the fixing of images on light-sensitive materials was the simultaneous but independent invention of the Frenchman Louis Daguerre and the Englishman William Henry Fox Talbot. News of their discoveries electrified Italy. "With this discovery man is no longer the sole painter of nature; she can now portray herself," wrote Gioacchino Belli; another, Cardinal Gioacchino Pecci (later Pope Leo XIII) expressed his amazement in verse:

> O shining image
> Imprinted by the sun's rays
> How well you reproduce
> the noble brow,
> The radiant eyes, the grace of visage.
>
> O wonderful power of the spirit
> O new marvel!
> Apelles who emulated Nature
> Could not paint a more perfect image.

Because early photographic emulsions required long exposures, it was impossible to capture the movement of figures or the changing effects of a moment in time. Stationary objects like buildings or townscapes were ideal subjects for early photographers, and these were just the images that were sought by tourists desiring souvenirs of their stay in Italy. Travel itself was changing in the mid-nineteenth century and the age of the true Grand Tour was coming to an end. The wealthier individual who stayed longer and brought home more expensive items like paintings and antique sculpture was now greatly outnumbered by middle-class tourists who had less time and less money to spend. The first group tour of Italy was conducted in 1864 by Thomas Cook, and popular guidebooks such as *Murray's Handbook*, Hillard's *Six Months in Italy*, and later *Baedekers* told the sightseer what to see and what to think at every turn. For such individuals, the purchase of inexpensive photographs was the perfect way to preserve their fleeting Italian experience.

As the market for documentary photographs increased, and as the new medium replaced painted and engraved *vedute*, the introduction of faster emulsions gradually permitted the inclusion of the moving figure. Photography subsequently came to seek more picturesque effects, with genre scenes occasionally commingled, as in earlier *vedute* by the Bamboccianti. Thus Gioacchino Altonbelli, experimenting with filters, concocted a *"Night" View of the Roman Forum*. With the advent of color emulsions in the twentieth century, the artfully idealized *veduta*, whose subtle monochromatism could be so suggestive, was supplanted by flashier images that tried to substitute the sensation of actuality for the reverie of contemplation. In this the photographic medium was perhaps the victim of its own success: as postcards proliferated, the idealized object, viewed with perfect concentration, virtually disappeared, and the quality of visual experience inevitably deteriorated.

Apathy is part of the price of conveniences. Mass tourism and the commercialization of Rome's cultural heritage have had similar numbing effects. James Joyce, a resident of Rome in 1906, was one of the first to confess to this particular twentieth-century malaise. In a letter to his brother, he complained about the number of tourists and souvenir sellers he encountered during a visit to the Forum. Gazing over the ruins, he was "so moved that I almost fell asleep....so I went home sadly. Rome reminds me of a man who lives by exhibiting to travelers his grandmother's corpse." More recently, Barbara Grizzuti Harrison confessed in her book *Italian Days* that, stepping into the Forum, she finds "the silence of the distant world deafening."

Have we lost our historical imagination? Or have we simply lost our own voices? The intensity of Brooke's gaze and the poetics of his visual expression are unusual among artists living in Rome. In an age that Lyotard characterized in *The Postmodern Condition* as being "incredulous toward meta-narratives," Brooke continues to believe in the myth of Rome. His work is coolly analytical, but it is tinged with wonder and unabashed enchantment with its subject. In his elegant monochromes, he continues to bear witness to the allure of the past.

More than four decades ago, Rose Macaulay defined that allure in *The Pleasure of Ruins*:

The ascendency over man's minds of the ruins of the stupendous past, the past of history, legend and myth, at once factual and fantastic, stretching back and back into ages that can be surmised, is half mystical in basis. The intoxification, at once heady and devout, is not the romantic melancholy engendered by broken towers and mouldered stones; it is the soaring of the imagination into the high empyrean where huge episodes are tangled with myths and dreams; it is the stunning impact of world history on its amazed heirs.

The most memorable Roman views have always been the product of a half-mystical intoxication of the senses and a soaring of the imagination. This was true of the paintings of Claude, the etchings of Piranesi, and of the photographs of Brooke. The majority of Brooke's views pay tribute to Piranesi's *Vedute di Roma* in both choice of site and viewpoint. In so doing he exposes the spatial exaggerations and structural distortions of his illustrious predecessor. But Brooke has no interest in portraying the beggars, boulevardiers, and colorful local populace that so intrigued Piranesi and most earlier *vedutisti*. By consciously suppressing the presence of the city's current inhabitants and its clamorous traffic, Brooke elevates his images above the experience of any particular moment. As a result, his pristine prints suggest a timelessness not unlike that achieved by the pioneering photographers of the mid-nineteenth century. Those early photographers, of course, could only dream of color emulsions, but Brooke deliberately chooses what he calls the "intellectual rigor of monochrome over the sensuous and seductive strengths of color." As a result, ephemeral distractions are further reduced and the impact of the image is concentrated.

Each small meditative view captures the grandeur of its subject. Grouped together, the series of two hundred photographs introduces us to a mythical city that spans the millennia from the early days of the Roman Republic to the last days of Mussolini. The streets in Brooke's *Views of Rome* may be empty and the piazzas eerily silent, but the mute stones speak. There is, as Macaulay suggests, something half-mystical in our contemplation of such a place. Brooke's Rome is ultimately a Rome of the imagination. Embracing a theme initiated by Foresti five hundred years ago, his sensibility is nonetheless contemporary, and it provides room for the viewer's imagination to wander. As we scrutinize the soaring arches, majestic porticoes, and awesome vistas of that monumental city, it is, in the end, our own nostalgia and longing that provides the color and atmosphere, the sound and the flavor of an authentic experience.

THE VEDUTE TRADITION

MALCOLM CAMPBELL

WHEN I ARRIVED AT THE AMERICAN ACADEMY IN ROME in October 1990, to assist at the opening of an exhibition of the *Views of Rome* by the great eighteenth-century graphic artist Giovanni Battista Piranesi, I had no idea that a fellow at the academy, Steven Brooke, was creating a photographic record of late-twentieth-century Rome inspired partly by centuries of similar projects, especially the enormous compendium of views of the city made by Piranesi. This was a serendipitous convergence of enterprises: as an art historian, it was a pleasure to see "our" Piranesi exhibition and catalog serve as an overture to Brooke's work.

The traditions of the *vedute* makers, particularly those of graphic artists such as Piranesi, play an important role in the formulation of Brooke's *Views of Rome*. However, his photographic views, made during his tenure at the American Academy in Rome, emulate rather than imitate the *vedutisti* tradition. The relationship is one of a respectful and knowledgeable dialogue. Brooke's goal as an artist is to acknowledge the tradition of the genre but also reshape it and extend it to accommodate the unique qualities of the photographer's art.

As such, it is appropriate that Brooke's work includes many architectural sites not depicted by Piranesi, especially the thirty-seven of modern Rome. Indeed, his views have an affinity with earlier photographic portraits of the city. At the very least, these earlier photographic campaigns are a reminder that the photographer's artistic options had already influenced the portrayal of Rome, and that these choices are in many respects quite different from those of the draftsman or painter.

Piranesi's *vedute* are characterized by 180-degree vistas, fusions of viewpoints from multiple elevations in a single image, and spatial manipulations of the structures represented. Unconstrained to a single viewpoint, he excised visible elements as it suited him and included others only visible when the site had been traversed. He thus presents us with an artificial image, one that is a highly satisfying but deceptive aide-mémoire that confirms in the aggregate the visitor's recollected perceptions of the monument rather than the site-specific view that a *veduta* implies. Piranesi's tricks of enlarging the small and exaggerating the already monumental, of lifting monuments high above the horizon line, of stretching piazzas, widening streets, and of dropping a wall or facade that interrupted a view are all part of the bag of tricks he shared with fellow *vedutisti*, but the audacity and skill with which he employed these techniques and with which he virtually sculpted with lights and darks the form

of the monuments, together with the sheer size of his etched plates, drastically exceeded the craft of his most ambitious competitor.

All this has a great deal to do with Brooke's photographic campaign. In eschewing color photography, he consciously separated his work from much of the vast photographic production of the late twentieth century and from aspects of the painted *vedute* of Rome with its five hundred years of artistic activity. Thus Brooke's monochrome photographs are directly related to those of the late nineteenth and early twentieth centuries and, above all, to the older traditions of graphic imagery, especially, and inevitably, the *vedute* of Piranesi.

The relationship between Brooke's *vedute* and those of his eminent predecessor, viewed in the context of the techniques of artistic production, resists the easy associations reflected in historical continuity and shared goals. The means of artistic production available to Brooke were not simply at variance with Piranesi's but often in opposition. The camera is single-lensed, and hence one-eyed, fixed upon a tripod located at a specific point in space. In contrast, the graphic artist's viewpoint is binocular, totally mobile and, of course, possesses sweeping peripheral vision. The camera, its aperture opened, accepts a single viewpoint and absorbs a single image. These qualities of the camera, antithetical to the methods of Piranesi, were intensified by Brooke, who deliberately elected not to employ currently fashionable panoramic or ultra-wide (and distorting) lenses. He further heightened these oppositions by choosing to frame his views directly through the camera, avoiding the temptation to use extensive darkroom manipulation and multiple-image montages.

There is also the question of time—the time during which the image recorded assumes its tangible, visible form. Although the darkroom offers opportunities for adjustment of detail, image texture, and tonality, it is the reception of the camera-recorded image on the film that is the primary trace upon which all subsequent modifications depend. The degree to which this trace can be adjusted while the image is being recorded is minimal, as is the actual time during which alterations can be effected in the darkroom. In contrast, the relative time frame in which Piranesi recorded his experience of a site was of potentially extraordinary duration. The fact that his surviving preparatory sketches are extremely summary and inscribed with notations of colors, materials, and atmospheric conditions suggests an approach that is similar to, if not identical with, the French impressionist capturing of "the moment." Indeed, his care to record the transitory conditions of sunlight and shadow and the transience of clouds (a feature seldom addressed by his predecessors) appears to support Piranesi's dedication to recording the essentially momentary. In actuality he transferred his sketches to the copper plates in his studio, and at this juncture his effects were realized through the time-consuming, labor-intensive process of the etcher's art. Just how far Piranesi's art is from shutter speeds and photographic print-development time is borne out by the assertion of his contemporary, J. G. Legrand, that the artist often made studies of the monuments he was preparing to etch both at high noon and under the full moon, further extending the time frame of his creative process. The paradox of this comparison of techniques is that Brooke's photographic prints, although far more instantaneous in their genesis, present us with images of such extraordinary stillness, silence, and permanence. Even his inclusion of a Piranesian sky and long shadows does not disrupt the seemingly immutable, iconic presence of the viewed monuments.

The potent effect of Brooke's images relative to those of the Piranesi *Vedute di Roma* series is particularly striking in view of their contrasting scale. The eighteenth-century artist was famous in his own time for the relatively enormous size of his etchings in this series (ca. 14 x 18 inches), which were approximately double the dimensions of his rivals' largest prints. In contrast, Brooke's prints eschew the nearly limitless capacity of the modern photographic enlarger. Measuring approximately a modest 5 x 7.5 inches, they are more similar in scale to Piranesi's earlier views of Rome, the *Piccole Vedute di Roma*. Unlike Piranesi's prints, which expand the traditional scale of the etched image as if to invade our space, Brooke's photographic prints are more intimate, intentionally drawing us into the spaces of the images they present.

By printing his *Views of Rome* in monochrome Brooke has erased the disruptive presence of modern urban furnishings and signage, and has marginalized that ubiquitous, most glaring element of the twentieth-century urban scene, the automobile. The avoidance of color also eases the entry of nineteenth- and twentieth-century architecture into the collection. Photographing at times when street and sidewalk traffic was minimal, but not altogether eliminated, has heightened the sense of seamless continuity with the *vedute* tradition without denying the contemporaneity of these new views.

It could be argued that Brooke's views omit our equivalents of Piranesi's street traffic, tourists, and street people. However, it must be admitted that some of Piranesi's most assertive urbanites, dressed in rags and wildly gesticulating, were surely caprices of their creator, more characters from the Italian comedy than bona fide inhabitants

of Rome. When the graphic tradition of *vedute* is explored, it is in fact true that most of its practitioners chose to portray the built environment, with minimal interest in the quotidian activities of the populace. This is the case of the views from the early Renaissance, by artists such as Maerten van Heemskerck, to the eighteenth century, typified by Piranesi's chief competitor, Giuseppi Vasi, in whose pictures the streets and piazzas, especially in the peripheral areas of Rome, appear, like Giorgio De Chirico's haunted views of imagined cities, preternaturally devoid of human activity. But we should recall that the city that never sleeps and is filled with commuters is a modern phenomenon; throughout earlier history the city contained dense concentrations of population only in those areas that functioned both as residence and workplace. Although some of the ancient and modern monuments of Rome have been located in these areas, the majority of its monuments have risen proudly and conspicuously in depopulated sectors of the city. The great monuments of Rome, even those built in Piranesi's time, more often than not slumbered in grand isolation. Janus-like, Brooke has used his photographer's art to record them as they now appear, yet he has elevated his views to timeless portraits in which the past endures in the present, where it is, after all, a precious and essential ingredient in the experience of Rome.

A PHOTOGRAPHIC VEDUTE DI ROMA
STEVEN BROOKE

THE SEVENTEENTH- AND EIGHTEENTH-CENTURY view painters and students of perspective, such as Vredemann deVries, established the compositional foundations for rendering architecture in any medium. As an architectural photographer, my artistic principles are strongly tied to that tradition. *Views of Rome* is the first collection of its kind on the city in over one hundred years, as well as the first to include monuments of the late nineteenth and twentieth centuries. It provides a link between those earlier traditions of architectural representation, now studied largely in an historical context, and a contemporary art based firmly on those traditions.

The best known of the view painters and engravers working in Rome, Giovanni Battista Piranesi, ennobled every monument and crumbling ruin he illustrated. Yet, as J. G. Links writes in *Townscape Painting and Drawing*, "No one ever saw Rome as Piranesi depicted it. And, in spite of the title he gave them, and masterpieces though they may be, [his] *Views of Rome* are not really views of Rome." John Wilton-Ely, in *The Mind and Art of Giovanni Battista Piranesi* observes that "the generation of early Romantics such as Goethe, brought up on such images, underwent a profound disillusionment on their initial encounter with the reality."

Despite centuries of criticism, Piranesi's images have served for generations as incomparable guides to Roman architecture. During my fellowship term at the American Academy in Rome, I traveled with his *Vedute di Roma, Antichità,* and *Piccole Vedute* in hand. Having always envied Piranesi's ability to rearrange visually piazzas, streets, and buildings, I sought to identify his specific vantage points to understand more fully both his alteration of perspective (to dramatically accentuate the scale of monuments) and his use of multiple viewpoints (to bring neighboring structures into a single composition). As a means of relating Piranesi's work directly to the specific concerns of architectural photography, I photographed over one hundred of those sites. In addition to the subjects of the Piranesi engravings, I also completed views of over one hundred other sites (some of which were depicted by Piranesi's contemporaries Vasi and Rossini) and over thirty views of modern Rome, for which there were surprisingly few, if any, high-quality photographs.

My ultimate goal was to create a *Views of Rome* for our own time. I learned quickly, however, how many overwhelming interventions have occurred since Piranesi worked in Rome. Wide, dangerous avenues have destroyed portions of the historic fabric, isolating monuments from one another. Tightly packed buildings and traffic circles have replaced the open fields that once surrounded the archi-

tecture and offered generous landscapes with which to frame views. Caravans of tourist buses, souvenir stands, and sprawling bus stations occupy the very locations from which we were meant to appreciate Rome's brilliantly designed church entrances. Widespread official paranoia, the inevitable result of senseless terrorist activities and the crush of tourists, precludes accessibility to many sites except through persuasion and stealth. There is now simply less room, less time, and less opportunity to work. These dramatic changes to the city demand new sensibilities and adjustments in modes of documentation. Lacking Piranesi's ability to reorder reality at will, such adjustments are difficult to achieve photographically without abandoning valued compositional systems or distorting scale and proportion. Ultimately, my challenge to develop an appropriate personal response to contemporary conditions was exactly the same one that Piranesi faced in the mid- eighteenth century.

THE PHOTOGRAPHS AND THE VEDUTE

I did not intend to merely imitate or replicate Piranesi's *vedute*. In fact, many of his architectural views would have been impossible to recreate. Either his positions were fanciful, created from the fusion of more than one position or from an invented vantage point, or contemporary buildings, foliage, and restoration activities interfered with that view. However, I often concluded that Piranesi's vantage points, irrespective of his subsequent manipulations, were the right ones for the conditions of his time. My goals were the same, whether or not our viewpoints coincided.

For several of his engravings, Piranesi used extremely wide angles of view with inevitable distortions of perspective: *S. Paolo Fuori le Mura* (p. 136), *Arco di Giano* (p. 68), *S. Pietro* (p. 128), *Colosseo* (p. 43), and *S. Maria degli Angeli* (p. 144). The characteristic "barrel" distortion in his *Colosseo* even suggests the use of a camera obscura with a primitive wide-angle lens. My photographs of these sites convey essentially the same information but avoid, where possible, any blatant distortion, especially in the foregrounds of interior views. The paradigm for these interior views is the work of the seventeenth-century Dutch painter Pieter Saenredam. Because of the low viewpoint, his paintings of vast church interiors include little or no foreground distortion. It is technically possible, of course, to include in one single image (even a distorted one) all that Piranesi included in his own. However, I did not consider fish-eye or ultra-wide panoramic lenses or multiple-image photomontage appropriate for this work.

In contrast to the straightforward and much less romantic depiction of his predecessors, Piranesi used dramatic and seamless multiple perspectives to provide "ideal" or "memorable" views. Further, in his *vedute* of *S. Paolo Fuori le Mura* (p. 137), *S. Maria degli Angeli* (p. 144), *S. Sebastiano* (p. 138), and the *Pantheon, Portico* (p. 49), Piranesi "removed" walls or columns to depict structures otherwise hidden. My photographs of these sites portray as much of the structure as possible from positions necessarily different than those of Piranesi. In his *Piazza del Quirinale* (p. 175), *Piazza di Spagna* (p. 167) and *Piazza del Popolo* (p. 166), he "moved" entire buildings to construct his views. When taken from analogous positions, the photographs indicate what Piranesi might have actually seen and demonstrate his manipulations of space and perspective to show important neighboring structures. In some cases, no single lens of any kind would encompass what Piranesi included in his image. Examples are *Tempio di Vesta* (p. 51), showing S. Maria in Priorata; *Foro di Augusto* (p. 40); *Grotta della Ninfa Egeria* (p. 89), showing the Church of S. Urbano; and the *Dio Rediculo* (p. 91), showing S. Urbano and the Grotto of Egeria.

Extensive restorations, excavations, erosions, or wholesale destruction of architectural segments have rendered many buildings and sites all but unrecognizable from the eighteenth-century *vedute*. Examples are *S. Paolo Fuori le Mura* (p. 136), the *Villa Sette Bassi* (p. 96), the *Porto di Ripetta* (p. 162), and the *Ripa Grande* (p. 163). In these cases, I chose positions analogous to those of the engravings to show what now exists and to offer a basis for comparison. In other instances the preferred view was blocked by contemporary buildings. When appropriate, I used compositional formulas similar to the original *vedute*: *Arco di Giano* (p. 68), *Terme di Diocleziano*, North Wall (p. 143), *Aquedotti Neroniani* (p. 79). For other locations, such as the *Tempio di Ercole Vincitore, Tivoli* (p. 101) and the *Tempio della Tosse, Tivoli* (pp. 102–103), my views are unrelated to the engravings.

Planning a photographic campaign in Rome means addressing changeable weather patterns, sun angles, tourists and traffic, restoration activities, the willingness of guards to allow access before and after operating hours or photography with a tripod, and other forces both unpredictable and exasperating. On Sundays, at least, the incessant Roman traffic diminishes, the piazzas are not used as parking lots, and the officious carabinieri are more relaxed in their pursuit of tripod-bearing photographers. At times, even my portfolio of officially stamped *permessi* were unconvincing, and I was forced to return when more sympathetic guards were on duty. However, I took some solace in knowing that no less a student of Rome than Goethe was once arrested for sketching.

Independent of Piranesi's choices, I selected times of day when the principal facades would be best illuminated. Piranesi's shadows, like his vantage points, are often invented. Occasionally, shadow and sky conditions coincided, as in the *Fontana dell'Acqua Felice* (p. 171), *S. Maria Loreto* (p. 147), and the interior of the *Canopo* (p. 109). I also worked with inclement weather and sky conditions that I would not ordinarily choose, often incorporating Rome's vast patches of clouds and palpable atmosphere in views such as the *Villa Sette Bassi* (p. 96) and the *Piramide di Caio Cestio* (p. 63).

MODERN ROME

No late-twentieth-century *Views of Rome* is complete without the architecture of the modern era (1850–1950). Many of these buildings have never been and are not now appreciated by either architectural critics or the Roman citizenry. Criticism has focused on their stylistic excesses (*Palazzo di Giustizia*, p. 194; *Il Vittoriano*, p. 202; *Ministero della Pubblica Istruzione*, p. 204), their austerity (*Palazzo della Civiltà Italica*, p. 222; *Palazzo Postale, Via Marmorata*, p. 212), or their original political patronage (*Foro Italico, E.U.R.*, pp. 218–223).

By depicting these buildings with the same respect shown for architecture of the earlier eras, I sought to foster a renewed appreciation at least of their historical significance if not of their architectural merit. I had hoped to include more examples of early modern rationalist-era architecture, but unfortunately, many of these buildings have been allowed to deteriorate into such disrepair and structural instability that they are isolated behind barbed wire and are completely inaccessible. Recent restoration activities in Garbatella (p. 208) and elsewhere, however, suggest that architecture of this era is finally gaining the attention it merits. Fortunately, the modernist buildings of the fascist-era new towns near Rome—Pontinia, Pomezia, Aprilia, Latina, and Sabaudia—have fared far better.

ARCHITECTURE AND PHOTOGRAPHY

Throughout his writings, John Ruskin, art critic and passionate watercolorist, stressed the faithful depiction of historic objects. Although Piranesi's representations are not the faithful documents Ruskin championed, he certainly shared Ruskin's sense of responsibility. In the often quoted preface to the first volume of *Antichità*, Piranesi wrote, "Seeing that the remains of the ancient buildings of Rome, scattered for the most part in gardens and fields, are being day by day reduced by the injuries of time or by the greed of their owners who, with barbarian license, secretly demolish them to sell the rubble for modern houses, I decided to preserve them in these plates." Except for such wholesale demolition, the injurious forces of his eighteenth century seem almost benign when compared to the ravages of our overpopulated, gasoline-powered twentieth century. In response, I share Piranesi's sense of personal involvement in the documentation of Rome.

Ruskin also reminded us that, "a nation's buildings must reflect and project its citizens' highest aspirations; buildings embody the sculpture and mouldings of the national soul. If the architecture of the present reflects a nation's highest values, so also does a nation's attitude toward its architectural heritage." The photography of architecture, whatever its initial purpose, also labors in service of that heritage—architecture is often studied and appreciated through photographs. When historic preservation efforts fail, as they too often do throughout the world, our architectural treasures are remembered *only* through photographs. Thus, the responsibility of contemporary architectural photography is not only genuine, but imperative. Thoughtful, dedicated, and disciplined photographic illustration can do justice to great architecture while rightfully sustaining on its own merits.

TECHNICAL NOTES

The compositional canons for depicting architecture are typically ignored by amateur and professional photographers alike. This is partially due to the ease with which automatic cameras make pictures. It is also the product of breathless contemporary journalism, which consumes rather than savors and rewards alacrity over contemplation—even in the documentation of architecture, where speed is rarely appropriate or necessary. The most important (and obvious) compositional principle is that the vertical lines of a building (or an interior) remain parallel to each other and to the picture plane. To have such control over the planes of a composition, it is necessary to use a view camera capable of complete perspective control. Without such controls, neither 35mm cameras nor even the optically excellent Hasselblads are adequate. Also critical are lenses that are specifically designed to avoid curvilinear ("barrel") distortion. For all my work, I use an Arca-Swiss 6 cm x 9 cm view camera. It has complete camera movements (swings, tilts, rises, and falls) at both the lens and film planes, and its controls are geared with microscopic precision. I use Schneider lenses with focal lengths from 47mm to 210mm. The 6 x 9 camera uses roll film rather than individually loaded sheet film. This facilitates experimentation, reduces setup and exposure times (often a critical consideration in locations like Rome), and increases productivity. Finally, the 2 x 3 proportion is more visually pleasing than the truncated 4 x 5 format. I used Kodak Tri-X black-and-white film, which has a broad tonal range that is ideal for the textured buildings of Rome.

I rendered my *Views of Rome* in monochrome to suppress the jarring and distracting effects of contemporary artifacts, which, particularly in color, conflict with a direct appreciation of the monuments. In monochrome, the monument and its context effectively dominate the view. Further, it visually integrates older buildings with newer ones, providing a more unified view of the city. Monochrome also facilitates comparisons with earlier *vedute* and photographs of other eras. I have used color to document contemporary architecture and am well aware of its seductive strengths and intellectual weaknesses. Color photography may be intriguing initially, but the literal quality of the medium leaves little room for the imagination. The Rome of memory and inspiration, the Rome that intoxicates and is addictive, is imprisoned by the stereotypical and mechanical response of even the best color film. Piranesi's engravings were designed to compete with the paintings of his day. His public, even that of our generation, has not seemed to miss the color.

FURTHER READING

Alpers, Svetlana. *The Art of Describing*.
Chicago: University of Chicago Press, 1983.

Atlas of Rome. Venice: Marsilio Editori, 1991.

Bayley, John Barrington. *Letarouilly on
Renaissance Rome*. New York: Architectural
Book Publishing Company, 1984.

Blunt, Anthony. *Guide to Baroque Rome*.
New York: Harper and Row, 1982.

Briganti, Giuliano. *The View Painters of Europe*.
London: Phaidon, 1970.

Campbell, Malcolm. *Piranesi: Rome Recorded*.
New York: Arthur Ross Foundation, 1989.

Clark, Eleanor. *Rome and a Villa*. New York:
Athenuem, 1952.

Coffin, David. *The Villa in the Life of Renaissance
Rome*. Princeton: Princeton University Press, 1979.

Cottino, Alberto. *Vedutisti*. Milan: Arnaldo
Mondadore Arti, 1991.

Crawford, Francis Marion. *Ave Roma Immortalis,
Vols. I and II*. New York: Macmillan, 1898.

Doordan, Dennis P. *Building Modern Italy: Italian
Architecture, 1914–1936*. New York: Princeton
Architectural Press, 1988.

Etlin, Richard A. *Modernism in Italian Architecture.
1890–1949*. Cambridge, Mass.: MIT Press, 1991.

Garofalo, Francesco, and Luca Veresani. *Adalberto
Libera*. New York: Princeton Architectural Press, 1992.

Goethe, Johann Wolfgang. Translated by W. H. Auden and
Elizabeth Mayer. *Italian Journey*. London: Penguin, 1962

Hawthorne, Nathaniel. *The Marble Faun*.
New York: Penguin, 1987.

Heydenreich, Ludwig, and Wolfgang Lotz. *Architecture in
Italy, 1400 to 1600*. Harmondsworth: Pelican, 1974.

Hibbert, Christopher. *Rome, The Biography of a City*.
London: Penguin, 1985.

James, Henry. *Italian Hours*. New York: Ecco Press, 1987.

Keaveney, Raymond. *Views of Rome, Thomas Ashby
Collection in the Vatican Library*. London: Scala
Publications, 1988.

Kostof, Spiro. *The Third Rome, 1870–1950: Traffic and
Glory*. Berkeley: University of California Press, 1973.

Kostof, Spiro. *A History of Architecture: Settings and Rituals*.
New York: Oxford University Press, 1985.

Krautheimer, Richard. *Rome, Profile of a City, 312–1308*.
Princeton: Princeton University Press, 1980.

Krautheimer, Richard. *Early Christian and Byzantine
Architecture*. 3d ed. Harmondsworth: Pelican, 1981.

MacDonald, William L. *The Architecture of the Roman
Empire. Vols. I and II*. New Haven: Yale University Press,
1982, 1986.

Meeks, Carroll L. V. *Italian Architecture, 1750–1914*. New
Haven: Yale University Press, 1966.

Origins of the Italian Veduta, The. Providence: Brown
University Exhibition Catalog, 1978.

Partner, Peter. *Renaissance Rome 1500–1559*.
Berkeley: University of California Press, 1976.

Portoghesi, Paolo. *Rome of the Renaissance*.
London: Phaidon, 1972.

Richardson, Lawrence, Jr. *A New Topographical Dictionary
of Ancient Rome*. Baltimore: The Johns Hopkins University
Press, 1992.

Rome in Early Photographs. Copenhagen: Thorvaldsen
Museum, 1977.

Rossi, Piero Ostilio. *Roma: Guida all'Architettura Moderna,
1909–1991*. Bari: Editore Laterza, 1991.

Varriano, John. *Italian Baroque and Rococo Architecture*.
New York: Oxford University Press, 1986.

Varriano, John. *Rome: A Literary Companion*.
London: John Murray, 1991.

Yourcenar, Marguerite. *Memoirs of Hadrian*. Translated by
Grace Frick. New York: Farrar, Straus & Giroux, 1963.

Ward-Perkins, John B. *Roman Imperial Architecture*.
2d ed. Harmondsworth: Pelican, 1981.

Watson, Wendy. *Images of Italy: Photography in the
Nineteenth Century*. South Hadley, Mass.: Mount Holyoke
College, 1980.

Wilton-Ely, John. *The Mind and Art of Giovanni Battista
Piranesi*. London: Thames & Hudson, 1988.

Wittkower, Rudolf. *Art and Architecture in Italy, 1600 to
1750*. 3d ed. Harmondsworth: Pelican, 1980.

TERME DI TRAIANO

ANCIENT ROME

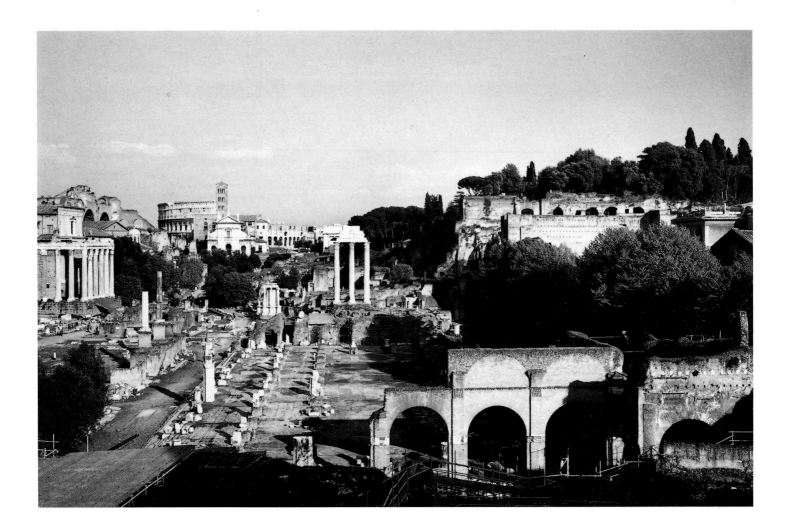

FORO ROMANO, OVERVIEW

This viewpoint from the Capitoline Hill has long been a favorite of artists. At the lower right are the arcades of the Basilica Giulia, 55 B.C. At the center are the three columns of the Temple of Castor and Pollux, fifth century B.C. (p. 29). At the left is the Temple of Antoninus and Faustina (p. 30); in the background are the Colosseum and the campanile of S. Maria in Cosmedin (p. 120). The Piranesi engraving (ca. 1746–1748) was drawn from a position between the Arch of Septimius Severus and the Temple of Vespasian. The photograph was taken further to the southwest.

FORO ROMANO

This view, taken from inside the Basilica Giulia, features the three Corinthian columns of the fifth-century B.C. Temple of Castor and Pollux. The wide pronaos was excavated in 1982–1985. The Temple of Antoninus and Faustina (p. 30) is at the left. Piranesi engraving, 1772.

TEMPIO DI ANTONINO E FAUSTINA

Emperor Antoninus Pius, the successor to Hadrian, dedicated this temple to his wife Faustina in
A.D. 141. When Antoninus died in 161, the Roman Senate rededicated the temple to them both.
Late in the eleventh century, the temple was converted into the church of S. Lorenzo in Miranda.
In 1536, the facade was recessed to allow the colonnade to be freestanding. The baroque facade was
added in 1602 when the church was rebuilt. Piranesi engraving, 1749–1750.

BASILICA DI CONSTANTINO

With its three enormous barrel-vaulted niches, and measuring 100 meters by 65 meters, the basilica is the largest monument in the Roman Forum. It was begun by Maxentius (306–310) and completed in the same century by Constantine. Its design inspired such Renaissance architects as Michelangelo who studied it while designing St. Peter's Dome. Bronze roof plates from the basilica were removed by Hororius I in 626 to cover St. Peter's. Both views depict the southwest facade facing the Roman Forum. Piranesi engraving, ca. 1749–1750.

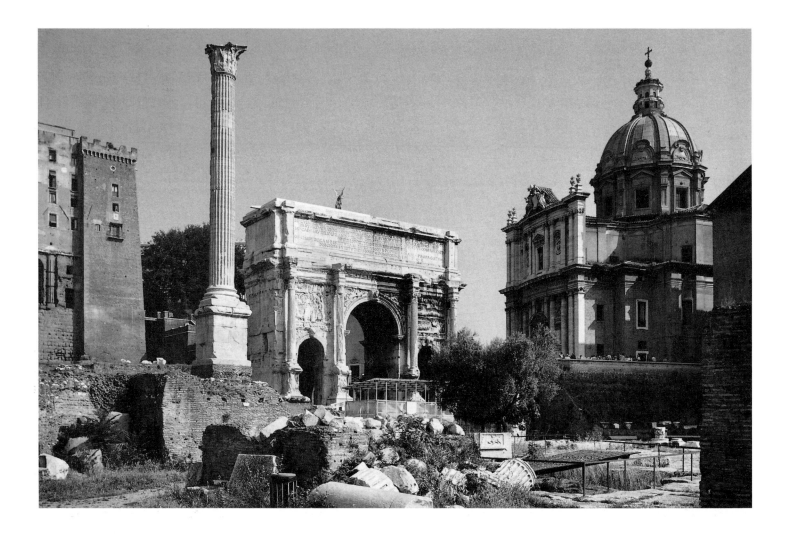

COLONNA DI FOCA, ARCO DI SETTIMIO SEVERO, SS. LUCA E MARTINA

The Column of Phocas, the last of the Forum monuments, was erected in 608 by Smaragdus to honor his centurion, Phocas, who had become Emperor of Byzantium. It also commemorated the emperor's gift of the Pantheon to Boniface IV. The 13.5-meter fluted Corinthian column was thought to have been taken from an imperial-era building. At the far left is a corner of the Palazzo Senatorio, built in 1143 on the ruins of the Tabularium, which dates from 78 B.C. The view is taken from the east looking west. Piranesi engraving, ca. 1749–1750.

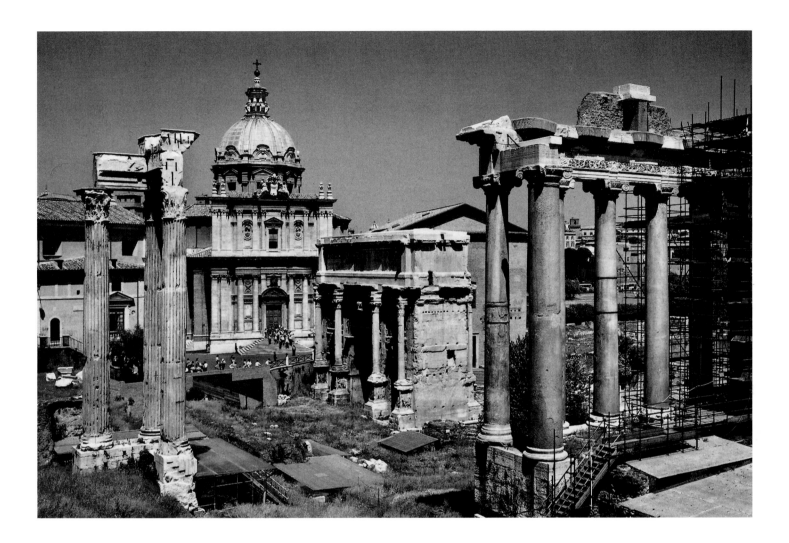

TEMPIO DI SATURNO, ARCO DI SETTIMIO SEVERO, SS. LUCA E MARTINA

This is one of the classic viewpoints of the Roman Forum. From left to right are the Temple of Vespasian (p. 39), the Arch of Septimius Severus (pp. 32, 34), the Temple of Saturn (p. 35), and the church of SS. Luca e Martina. The church was built in the seventh century on the site of the Senate Archives. The facade was designed by Pietro da Cortona in 1634, following the discovery of a sarcophaguscontaining the remains of S. Martina.

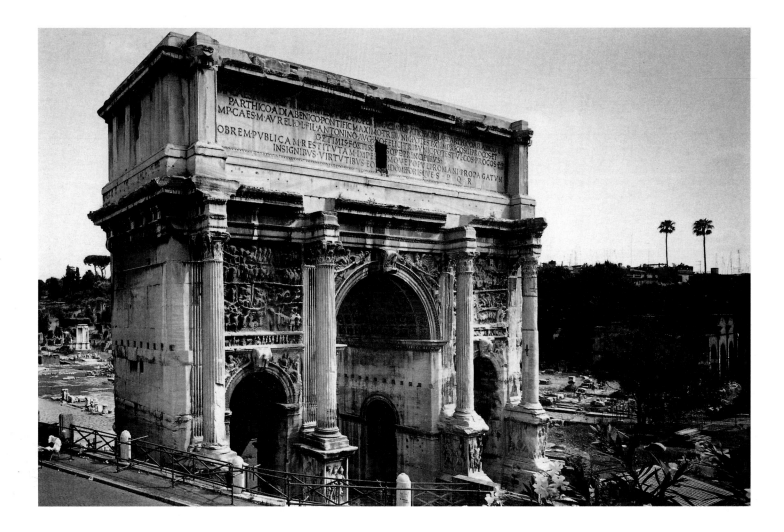

ARCO DI SETTIMIO SEVERO, WEST FACADE

Erected in 203, this arch was dedicated to Septimius Severus and his sons, Caracalla and Geta. It celebrated the victories of Septimius Severus over the Parthians, Arabs, and the Adiabenians of Assyria and his formation of the new province of Mesopotamia. Caracalla removed Geta's name after murdering him. The arch is nearly 21 meters high, more than 23 meters wide, and faced with marble. Four detached Corinthian columns form a false portico. Piranesi engraving, 1772.

TEMPIO DI SATURNO

It is thought that this temple, one of the oldest in the Roman Forum, was originally built in 498 B.C. to honor the god-king of Italy. It was rebuilt by Plancus in 42 B.C., restored in 283, and again in about 400. The podium and eight columns date from the fifth century. The Ionic capitals were part of the fifth-century restoration. The Temple of Saturn was also used as a state treasury. At the left of the photograph (the right edge of the engraving), is the Arch of Septimius Severus. Both images depict the north elevation of the temple. Piranesi engraving, 1774

TEMPIO DI CASTORE E POLLUCE

This view toward the south shows, on the left, the three columns of the Temple of Castor and Pollux. To their right is the Temple of Divine Augustus. Further right are the remains of the Basilica Giulia, begun by Caesar in 54 B.C. and completed by Augustus. Piranesi engraving, ca. 1749–1750.

TEMPIO DI VENERE E ROMA

The Temple of Venus and Rome is located at the eastern end of the Roman Forum, on the site of the vestibule to Nero's Domus Aurea. Begun by Hadrian in 121 to honor Venus and Roma Aeternae, it was the largest temple in Rome, measuring 100 meters by 53 meters. It was dedicated in 135, damaged by fire in 283, and restored in 307 by Maxentius. It was the last active pagan temple in Rome until it was closed in 391 by Theodosius, remaining intact until 625 when Honorius I removed the bronze roof tiles for the Baldacchino in St. Peter's. Both images depict the *cella* dedicated to Venus. Piranesi's engraving (ca. 1748–1749) also depicts the apse dedicated to Roma, which cannot actually be seen from this vantage point.

FORO E MERCATI DI TRAIANO

Five imperial forums occupy the area between the Roman Forum and the Quirinale: the Forums of Augustus (pp. 40, 41), Caesar, Vespasian, Nerva (p. 42), and Trajan. Mussolini built the Via Fori Imperiale, which ran through this area and over the Forums of Vespasian and Nerva, destroying many sixteenth-century buildings. The Forum of Trajan was built between 107–113 and was the last of the great imperial forums. The markets were built in the early second century on the slope of the Quirinal Hill. The semicircular arrangement housed three stories of 150 individual shops. Piranesi engraving, ca. 1756.

TEMPIO DI VESPASIANO

Located at the far west end of the Roman Forum, the Temple of Vespasian was built by the emperor's sons, Titus and Domitian, following his death in A.D. 79. The frieze consists of priestly insignia: cap, sprinkler, pitcher, sacrificial knife, patera, saucer, ladle, and ax. The columns were excavated in 1811 by Valdier. In the center of the image are the columns of the Portico of the Die Consentes, the last pagan monument, built in 376 by Vettius Praetextatus. Piranesi engraving, 1753–1754.

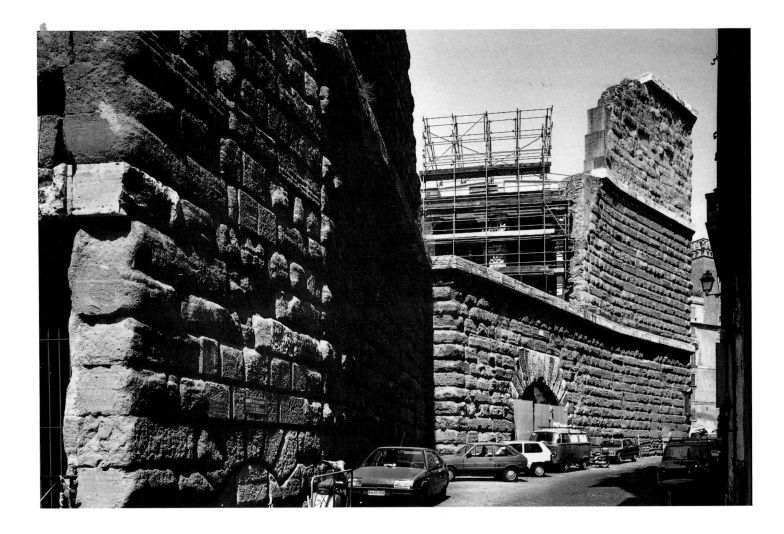

FORO DI AUGUSTO, EAST WALL

Begun in 37 B.C. and completed in A.D. 2, the forum was built to commemorate the victory of Philippi in 42 B.C. The three Corinthian columns of the Temple of Mars Ultor (under restoration) are seen through a break in the large wall that was designed to separate the forum from the surrounding ancient Subura district of the Quirinale. Piranesi's engraving (1756–1757) shows more of the wall than can actually be seen from this position and places the Arch of Pantani closer to the church of SS. Quirico e Giuletta (far right) than is the case.

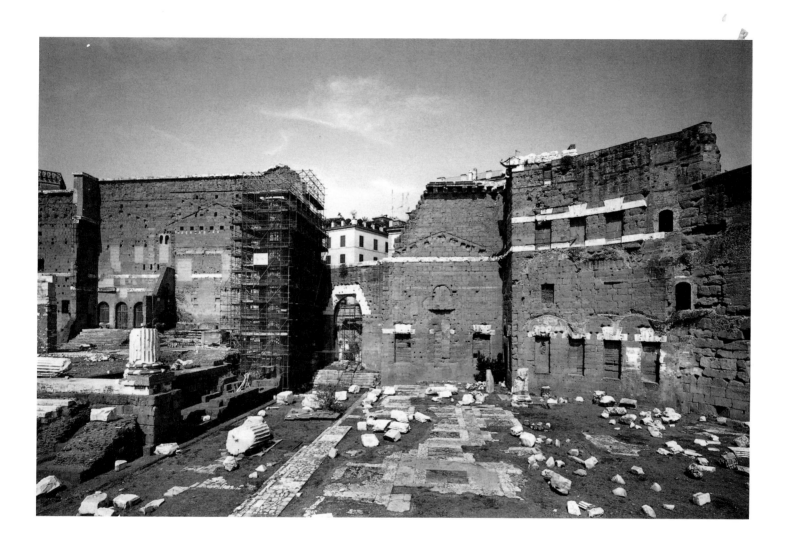

FORO DI AUGUSTO

The Forum of Augustus was the second of the imperial forums. The original site extended from the back wall (p. 40) to the Roman Forum. The modern Via Fori Imperiali now runs through and over it. The three columns belong to the Temple of Mars Ultor (the Avenger) and have been under restoration for many years. To the right are the remains of the southern exedra of the basilica. Piranesi engraving, ca. 1756.

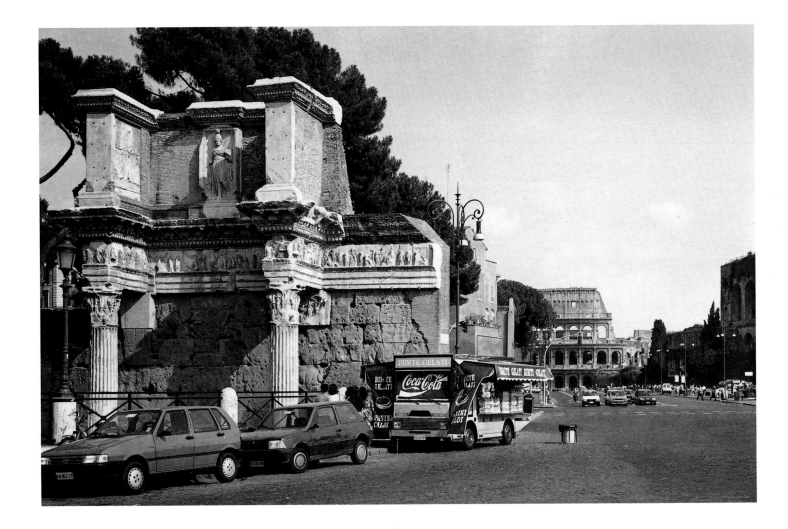

FORO DI NERVA

Located at the south end of the Forum of Augustus (p. 41), the Forum of Nerva was begun by Domitian and completed by Nerva in A.D. 97. It connected the Subura Quarter to the Forum of Vespasian and was thus called the Forum Transitorium. Paul V removed marble from the Temple of Minerva for the Fontana dell'Acqua Paola; only two Corinthian columns remain. The frieze of the entablature depicts activities of Minerva. In the distance is the Colosseum. Both the photograph (with the ever-present lunchwagon) and the 1770 Piranesi engraving (with its indecorous animals) depict the eternally profane activity of this area.

COLOSSEO, ARCO DI CONSTANTINO

In A.D. 72, on the lake of Nero's Golden House, Vespasian built the largest Roman amphitheater in the world. The name (*colosseo*, in Italian) came either from the 35-meter-high statue of Nero that stood to the west, or the actual size of the building itself, 527 meters in diameter and 57 meters high. The views in both the photograph and the 1761 Piranesi engraving are from the Esqualine Hill. Like Piranesi's view of the Arch of Janus (p. 68), the extreme curvilinear distortion at the center of his engraving suggests the use of a camera obscura with a wide-angle lens.

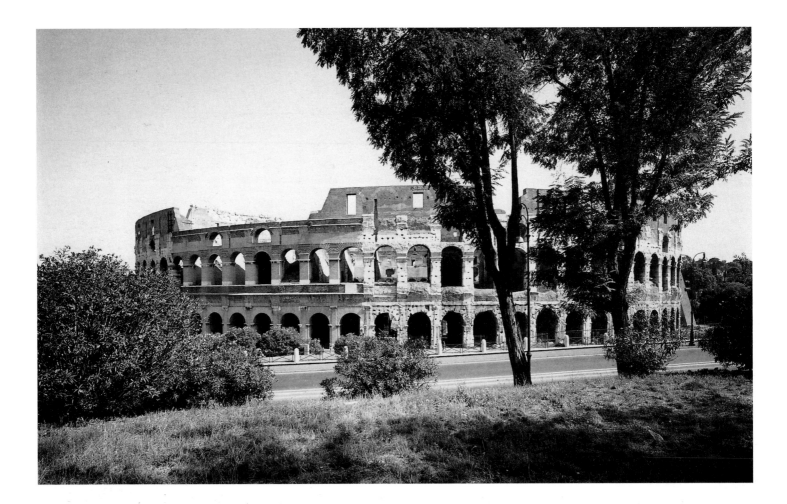

COLOSSEO, SOUTHWEST FACADE

This view is from the elevated Parco del Celio, immediately northwest of the Temple of Claudius.
The 1776 Piranesi engraving is a remarkably invented "aerial view."

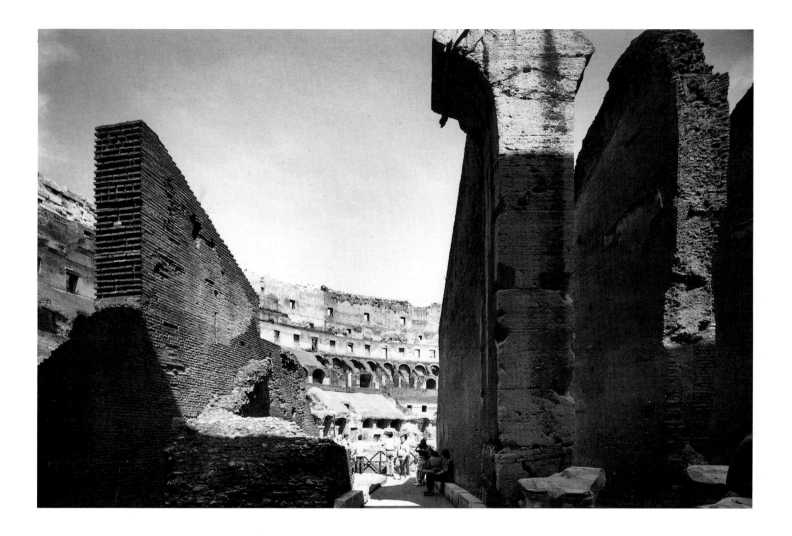

COLOSSEO, INTERIOR

In the fourteenth century, the Colosseum was treated as a travertine quarry for, among other sites, the Farnese Palace. This practice was halted by Benedictus XIV (1470–1458), who declared the Colosseum sacred to the memory of the martyred Christians. The arena measures 76 meters by 43 meters and could hold 50,000 spectators. Both the photograph and the 1766 Piranesi engraving look northeast toward the largest of the remaining walls. The photograph was taken from further within the structure.

ARCO DI CONSTANTINO

Constantine built this arch in 315 to commemorate his victory over Maxentius at Ponte Molle (p. 67). Like several other fourth-century buildings, it was partially constructed of fragments of second-century monuments. The arch was restored to its present condition in 1804. The Temple of Venus and Rome (p. 37) are at the left. The view is of the southwest facade from a position on the Via S. Gregorio. The Meta Sudans, a fountain built by Titus but destroyed by Mussolini in 1936, is seen through the central arch in the 1771 Piranesi engraving.

PIAZZA ROTONDA, PANTHEON

Many consider the Piazza Rotonda to be the very center of Rome, and the Pantheon (also pp. 48, 49) the city's finest architectural structure. Clement XI enlarged the piazza in 1711, commissioning Fillippo Barigioni to add the base for the Obelisk of Ramses the Great, which came to the site from nearby Piazza San Ignazio. Alexander VII lowered the level of the piazza to provide a better view of the architecture. The base of the fountain was built by Giacomo della Porta in 1575. Piranesi's engraving (ca.1746–1748) exaggerates the size of the piazza.

PANTHEON

One of the world's architectural masterpieces, the Pantheon is the best preserved monument of ancient Rome. Its austere beauty and harmonious proportions have influenced architects for centuries. Built by Agrippa in 27 B.C., the building was damaged by fire in A.D. 80. Hadrian rebuilt it between 118–128, orienting it to the north. Bonaface IV consecrated it as a church in 609. During the reign of the first Christian emperors, it was abandoned and was then pillaged by the Goths. In the 1620s, Urban VIII melted down the bronze ceiling of the portico for the Baldacchino at St. Peter's. Alexander VII commissioned Bernini to add two incongruous turrets that were later removed in 1883. Piranesi engraving, 1761.

PANTHEON, PORTICO

The portico is 34 meters wide, 15.5 meters deep, and supported by 16 monolithic Corinthian columns 12.5 meters high and 4.5 meters in diameter. The capitals and bases are white marble. The eastern end of the portico collapsed in the mid-sixteenth century and was rebuilt by Urban VIII. In his 1769 engraving, Piranesi "rearranged" the columns to establish his somewhat misleading view.

TEMPIO DELLA FORTUNA VIRILE

Located in the Forum Boarum, the ancient cattle market, this Republican-era Greco-Roman temple dates from the late second century B.C. Four well-restored fluted Ionic columns stand in front of the portico. It was consecrated in 872 and later dedicated to S. Maria Egiziaca in the sixteenth century. The temple was restored to its antique form in the early twentieth century. In the center of both the photograph and the 1750–1751 Piranesi engraving are S. Maria in Cosmedin (p. 120), and, to the right, the Temple of Vesta (p. 51).

TEMPIO DI VESTA

This little temple in the Forum Boarum is believed to be the oldest marble edifice in Rome. It dates from the first century B.C. and is now believed to have been dedicated to Hercules Victor. The name Vesta refers to the earlier belief that the temple was dedicated to Vesta, goddess of the circular hearth. In the middle ages, it was converted to the Church of S. Stefano della Carrozze and, in 1560, was rededicated to S. Maria della Sole. Piranesi engraving, 1753–1754.

ANFITEATRO CASTRENSE

The amphitheater is located east of Porta S. Giovanni (p. 158) on Viale Castrense, just west of S. Croce in Gerusalemme (p. 141). It is thought to have been built as a private amphitheater by either Emperor Heliogobalus (218–222) or Alexander Severus (222–235). It was incorporated into the Aurelian Wall by Honorius (395–423). The view in both the photograph and the 1745 Piranesi engraving is of the southwest quadrant seen from Viale Castrense.

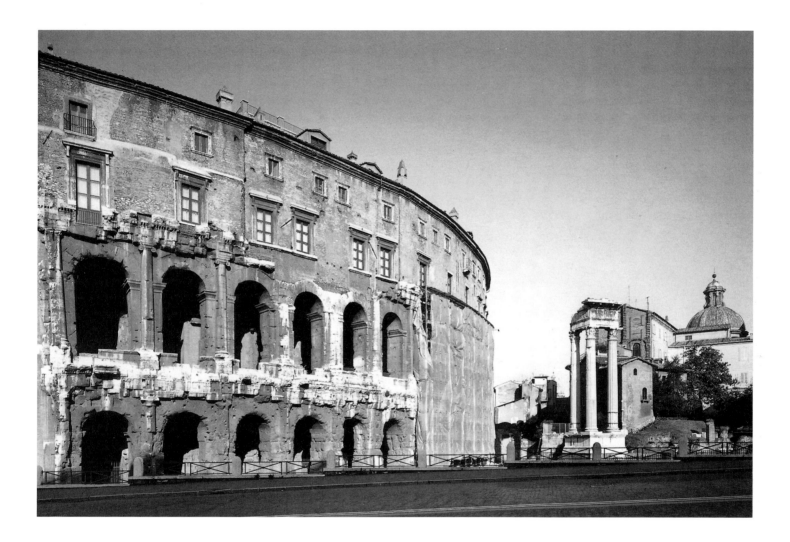

TEATRO MARCELLO

The Teatro Marcello was built by Augustus and dedicated to his nephew, Marcello, who died in 23 B.C. Restored in the sixteenth century by Peruzzi, its superimposed arcades were influential in Renaissance design. Doric columns appeared on the ground level, Ionic on the second, and Corinthian (which no longer exist) above. The Orsini family built their palace over the remaining antique arcades. The photograph includes the columns of the Temple of Apollo (443 B.C.) and the dome of S. Maria in Campitelli. Piranesi engraving, ca. 1749.

MAUSOLEO DI AUGUSTO

Augustus, the first emperor of Rome, built this monumental sepulcher for his family and himself. It was covered in white marble and surrounded by a raised platform planted with trees. The tomb was sacked in the middle ages and converted into a fortress by the Colonna family. In the seventeenth century, it was used as an amphitheater and, until 1936, as a concert hall. It is surrounded by the Piazza Augusto Imperatore, one of the worst examples of fascist town planning. Piranesi engraving, ca. 1762.

HADRIANIUM

Located in the Piazza di Pietra, the Hadrianium, or Temple of Hadrian, was built in 145 by Antoninus Pius (138–161) and dedicated to his father, Hadrian. The surviving eleven fluted Corinthian columns, originally freestanding, are 15 meters high. In 1695, Innocent XII had Carlo Fontana convert it into the Dogana di Terra (Customs House). Piranesi engraving, 1751–1753.

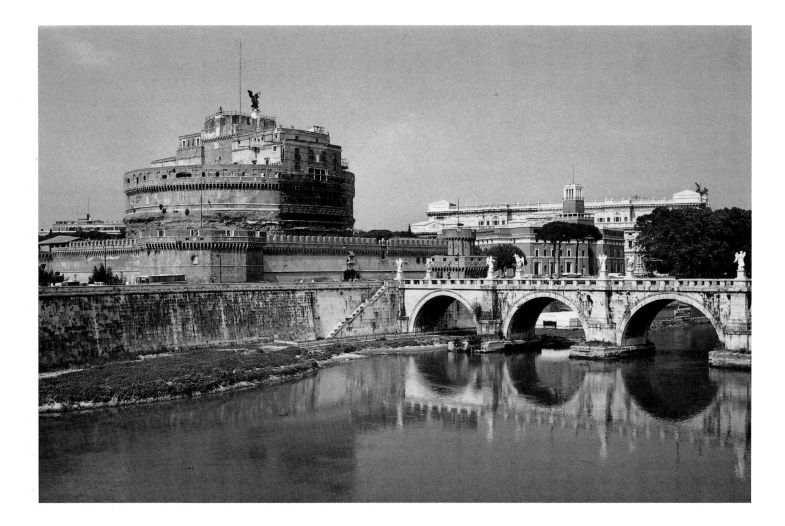

CASTEL E PONTE S. ANGELO

For centuries, this view showing the Castel S. Angelo and the Ponte S. Angelo has served as a signature view of Rome for artists. Piranesi engraving, ca. 1756.

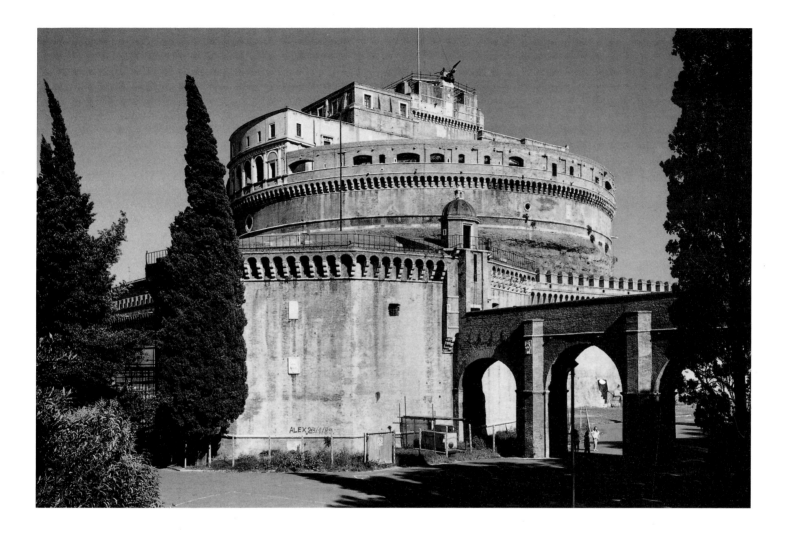

CASTEL S. ANGELO

Begun in A.D. 135 by Hadrian as a mausoleum for his family, this tomb eventually contained the funerary urns of all the emperors from Hadrian to Septimius Severus. In its colorful and varied history, this fortresslike structure has been a fortified military stronghold, a barracks, and a jail. The 84-meter base is topped by a 20-meter-high drum. The arcaded, covered passage to the right leads to the Vatican Palace. It is from the parapet of Castel S. Angelo that Puccini's Tosca leaps to her death. Piranesi engraving, 1755–1756.

COLONNA DI TRAIANO

Dedicated in A.D. 113, the 39.8-meter column commemorates Trajan's victory over the Dacians (now Romania). It is considered the masterpiece of Roman sculptural art. It depicts 100 scenes with 2,500 figures in relief spiraling 200 meters up the column. Ignoring the ancient stricture against burial within the city, Trajan had his ashes interred in the base. In 1587, Sixtus V replaced the bronze statue of Trajan with one of St. Peter. The foreground columns are from the Basilica Ulpia; to the right is SS. Nome di Maria (p. 147). Piranesi engraving, ca. 1748–1749.

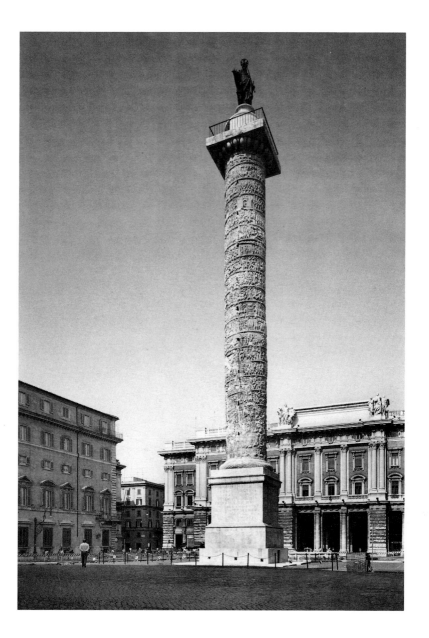

COLONNA DI MARCO AURELIO

Erected by the Roman Senate between A.D. 180–193, the column commemorates the emperor's victories over the Germans and Sarmatians in the Danube. It is formed from 27 blocks of marble and stands 29 meters; including base and statue, it is 42 meters high. In 1589, Sixtus V replaced the statue of the emperor with one of St. Paul. To the left is the Palazzo Chigi; behind the column stands the Galleria Colonna (p. 206). Piranesi engraving, ca. 1748–1749.

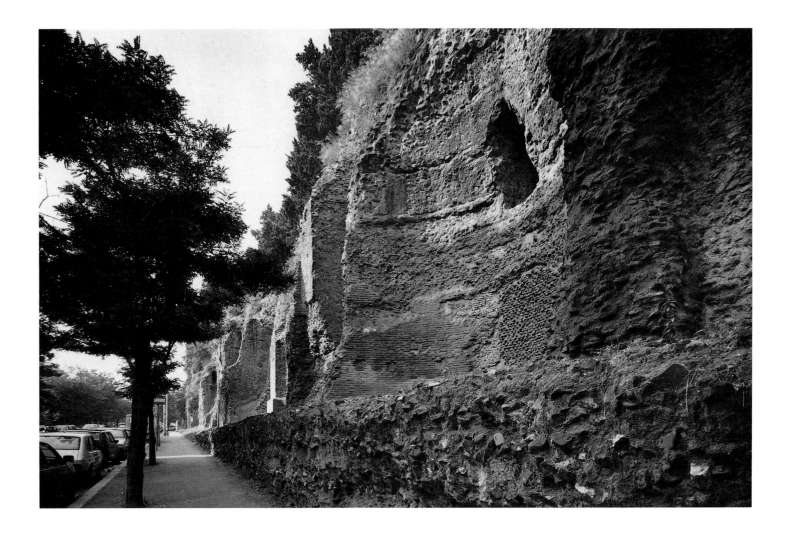

TEMPIO DI CLAUDIO

In A.D. 54 Agrippina, Nero's mother, dedicated this temple to her fourth husband, Claudius. Nero later converted it into a nymphaeum for his Domus Aurea. It was rebuilt by Vespasian in 69. Piranesi engraving, ca. 1756.

TEMPIO DI CLAUDIO, SUBSTRUCTURE

Beside the convent of the Church of SS. Giovanni e Paolo (p. 124), part of the two-story substructure of the Temple of Claudius is visible. Piranesi engraving, 1750–1751.

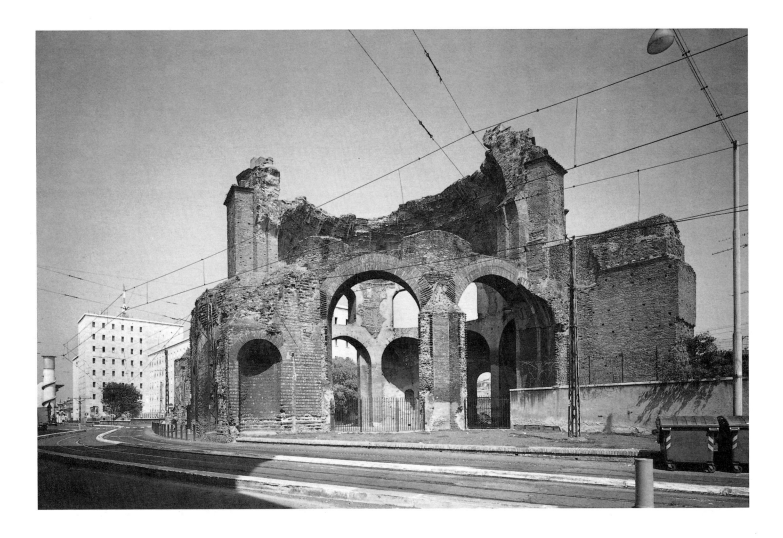

TEMPIO DI MINERVA MEDICA

Surrounded by train tracks and streetcar wires on the Via Giovanni Giolitti, northwest of Porta Maggiore (p. 74), is the unique ten-sided Temple of Minerva Medica. It owes its name to a statue of Minerva and a serpent that was found on the site. It is now thought that the Temple is actually a third- to fourth-century nymphaeum from the Gardens of Licinius. The cupola, which can be seen in the Piranesi engraving (ca. 1764), collapsed in 1828.

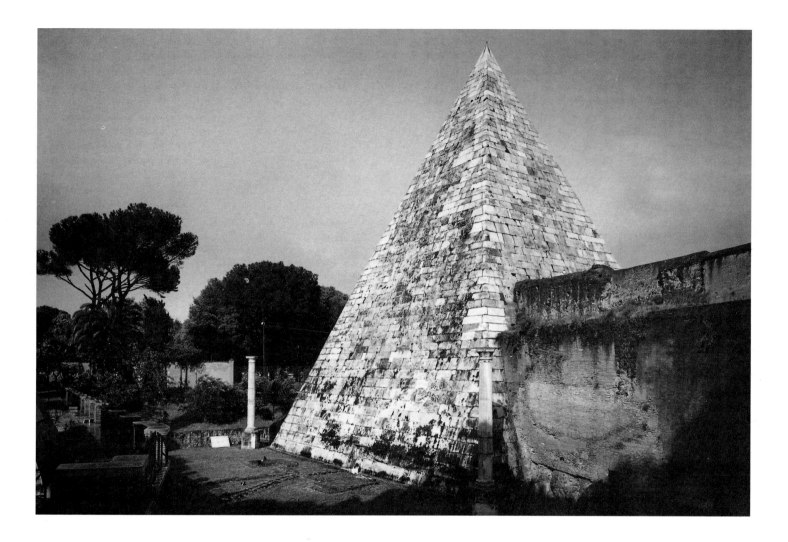

PIRAMIDE DI CAIO CESTIO

Caius Cestius was an Augustan-era praetor and tribune of the plebes. A Roman citizen (not an emperor), he died in 12 B.C. His marble-covered tomb, located adjacent to the Protestant Cemetery, is 27 meters high with a 22-meter square base. It was included in the Aurelian Wall in the third century. Both views display the north and west facades. Piranesi engraving, 1761.

ISOLA TIBERINA

The traditional image of Tiber Island evokes a ship in the middle of the Tiber. In keeping with the maritime symbolism, the tenth-century Church of S. Bartolomeo (p. 122) was oriented with the apse toward the southern end—or "prow"—of the island. To the right is the Ponte Fabricio (p. 65). Piranesi engraving, 1775.

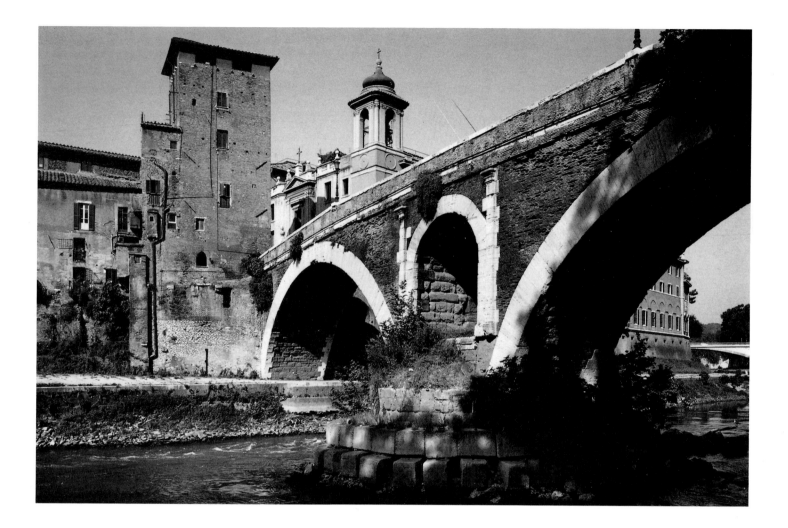

PONTE FABRICIO

The Ponte Fabricio is the oldest Roman bridge in the city, serving pedestrian traffic to the Isola Tiberina. Built by Fabricius in 62 B.C., it is also called the Ponte "Dei Quattro Capi" after the four-headed Janus on the parapet. In the background on the left are towers from S. Bartolomeo; on the right, a portion of the hospital of the Fatebenefratelli (founded in 1548). The photograph and the engraving depict the southeast facade. Piranesi engraving, ca. 1756.

PONTE NOMENTANO

The Via Nomentana follows the path of the ancient Roman road to Nomentum (now Mentana), about 20 km northeast of Rome. In the Quartiere de Monte Sacro, it crosses the River Aniene at the Ponte Nomentano. The ancient bridge was rebuilt in 552 by Narses and restored again by Nicholas V in 1447–1455. It is believed that here, in 800, the historic meeting between Leo III and Charlemagne took place prior to the latter's coronation. Although surrounded by vegetation, the bridge is still accessible. Both the photograph and the 1754 Vasi engraving depict the north side of the bridge. The fifteenth-century crenelated tower remained until 1829.

PONTE MOLLE (MILVIO)

A bridge has stood at this location ever since the first one was built in 109 B.C. Nicholas V remodeled the bridge in the fifteenth century, adding the watchtowers. Pius VII remodeled it again in 1805, adding a triumphal arch designed by Valadier. Garibaldi demolished it in 1849 to impede the French advance, but Pius IX promptly restored it in 1850. The bridge is best remembered as the site where Constantine defeated Maxentius in 312. Piranesi engraving, 1762.

ARCO DI GIANO

Located east of the Forum Boarum and adjacent to S. Giorgio in Velabro (p. 123), the Arch of Janus dates from the fourth century, possibly from Constantine's reign. The name derives from the god Janus, protector of road junctions. The arch is partially constructed of ancient fragments with sculpture niches on all sides. This photograph depicts the north and west elevations of the arch and the tower of S. Giorgio in Velabro. The 1771 Piranesi engraving depicts the Arch of the Moneychangers on the left and the north and east elevations of the arch. Piranesi's depiction is among his more exaggerated views, with a distortion of the corner of the arch closest to the viewer.

PORTICO DI OTTAVIA

The Portico of Octavia was built by the Roman general Octavius in the second century B.C. and restored by Octavian in 33 B.C. It was erroneously attributed to Octavia, sister of Octavian, and it was this popular dedication that Piranesi cites in his *veduta*. The portico was restored again by Septimius Severus in A.D. 203, and his inscription appears on the entablature. The Church of S. Angelo in Pescheria, restored in 1700, is at the right. The portico has served both heraldic and commercial functions since antiquity and was a gateway to the marketplace in the heart of the Jewish Ghetto. Piranesi engraving, ca. 1750–1751.

MURE AURELIANE

The Emperor Aurelian constructed new walls to defend Rome against the increasing danger of barbarian invasion and to defend the newer settlements outside the old Servian Walls. The new walls included the Janiculum and Pincian hills. Begun in A.D. 270, they were completed in 282 and were over 18,000 meters long with 16 gates and 383 towers. Honorius restored them between 402–403, as did many popes who followed. This section is near the Porta S. Paolo (p. 72).

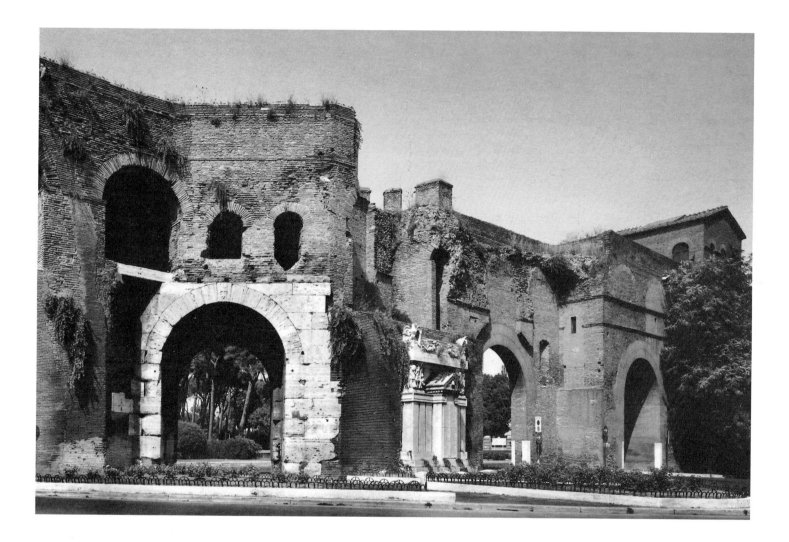

PORTA PINCIANA

This gate marks the terminus of the beautiful tree-lined Via Veneto. It was built around 403 by Honorius and fortified in the sixth century by Belisarius, Justinian's famous general. Vasi engraving, 1747.

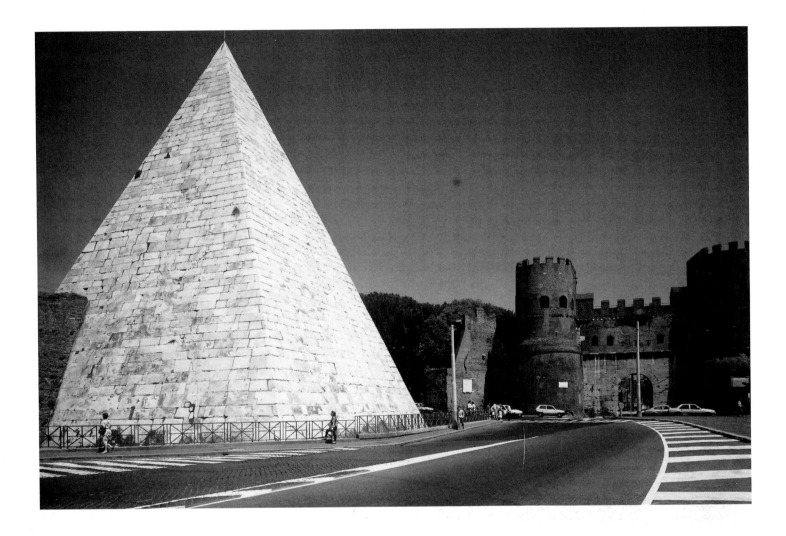

PORTA S. PAOLO, PIRAMIDE DI CAIO CESTIO

The Pyramid of Caius Cestius (p. 63) was incorporated into the Aurelian Wall in the third century. The wall also joins the Porta S. Paolo, the ancient Porta Ostiensis that leads to the port city of Ostia. The gate was rebuilt by Honorius in 402 and is the only one of Aurelian's (A.D. 270–275) gates that has remained intact. Piranesi engraving, 1756.

PORTA S. SEBASTIANO

Formerly the Porta Appia, this is the largest and best preserved gate in the Aurelian Wall. It was rebuilt by Honorius in the fifth century and again by Belisarius in the sixth century. The interior of the towers now contains a Museum of the Walls. The photograph is of the south facade, from the Via Appia Antica looking back toward the city. Rossini engraving, 1829.

PORTA MAGGIORE

Built by Claudius in A.D. 54, the Porta Maggiore, or Porta Prenestina, is formed by archways of the Acqua Claudia and the Anio Novus (aqueducts begun by Caligula in A.D. 38 and completed in 52). The Via Prenestina (to the left) and the Via Casilina (the ancient Via Labicana) have always passed through the Porta Maggiore. The gate was part of the Aurelian Wall and was restored in 405 by Honorius (395–423). Both the 1775 Piranesi engraving and the photograph show the western facade, from inside the wall. Just beyond the center pier is the curious travertine Tomb of the Baker, ca. 51 B.C.

PORTA LATINA

The Porta Latina was one of the original gates in the Aurelian Wall. The tower on the left is believed to date from that period. The Porta Latina was rebuilt by the Emperor Honorius at the beginning of the fifth century, and again in the sixth century by Belisarius, who constructed the cylindrical tower on the right. The views are from outside the gate. Vasi engraving, 1747.

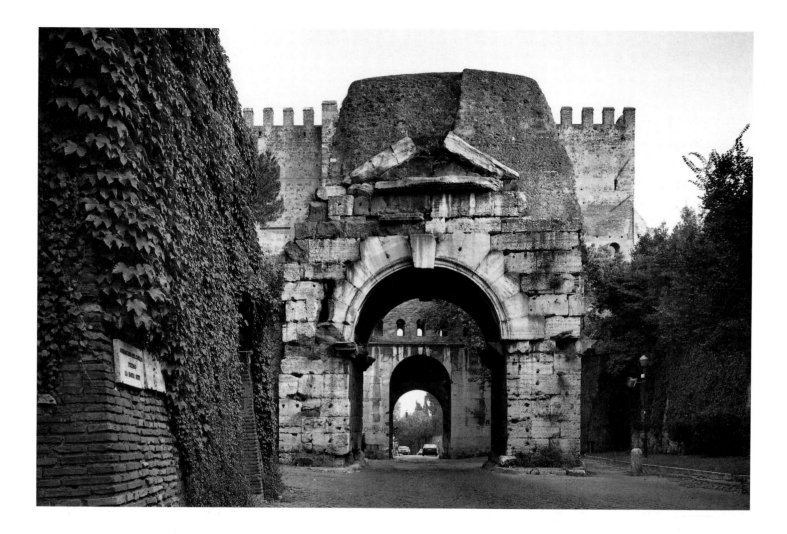

ARCO DI "DRUSO"

The Arch of "Drusis" is located on the north side of the Porta S. Sebastiano (p. 73). It is believed that the arch was built not in honor of Drusis, the younger brother of the emperor Tiberius, but rather to support the aqueduct carrying waters over the Via Appia to the Baths of Caracalla. The arch dates from the second century A.D. Piranesi engraving, 1745.

ARCO DI DOLABELLA E SILANO

An inscription above the arch originally indicated that the arch was built in 40 B.C. by Consuls Dolabella and Silanus, possibly as an entrance to a military exercise field on the Coelian Hill. Nero employed the arch to support his aqueduct.

FONTANA DELL'ACQUA GIULIA

Emperor Alexander Severus (222–234) built this nymphaeum as the terminus for the waters from the Acqua Giulia. The ruins stand in a corner of the much-neglected Piazza Vittorio Emanuele. It was called "Trophies of Marius" because the trophies commemorating Domitian's first-century conquest of the Germans once stood there. The trophies were removed in the sixteenth century and relocated to the Capitoline Museum (p. 173). Piranesi engraving, 1751–1753.

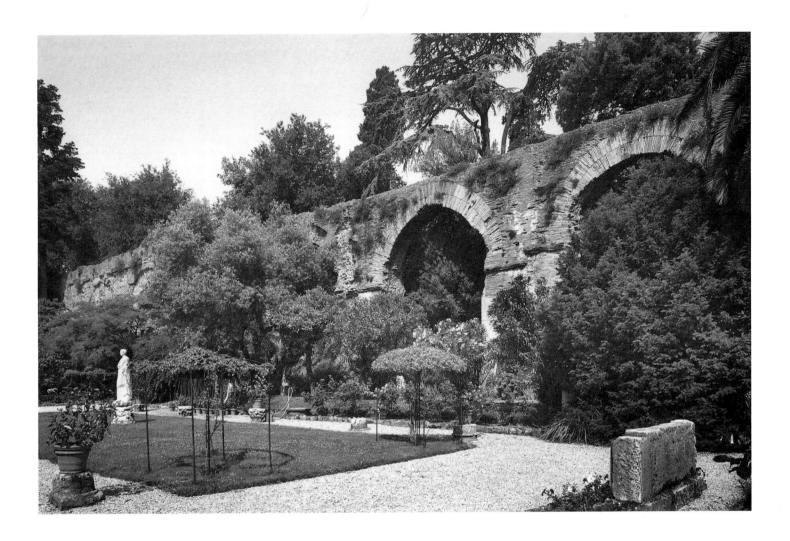

AQUEDOTTI NERONIANI

Nero's aqueducts drew waters from the Acqua Claudia to the Domus Aurea, the artificial lakes of the Colosseum, as well as to reservoirs for the Palatine and Aventine. Part of the structure is visible from the Arch of Dolabella (p. 77). This section of the aqueduct is located on the grounds of the Villa Wilkonsky, now a part of the British Embassy. The photograph shows the south facade from inside the villa. The 1775 Piranesi engraving depicts the north facade, the villa on the right.

TERME DI TRAIANO

These ruins were often referred to, even by Piranesi, as the Baths of Titus because of an incorrect association with a basin from those baths. The Baths of Trajan were built over Nero's Domus Aurea (Golden House). This view is of the northwest facade of one of the central exedra in the complex. Piranesi engraving, 1776.

TERME DI TRAIANO, EXEDRA

Piranesi's 1775 engraving offers a bird's-eye view of the Baths of Trajan, looking from the north-east to the southwest. This particular ruin, the southwest exedra, corresponds to the structure in the upper right of his engraving.

AQUEDOTTI DELL'ACQUA CLAUDIA, COMPAGNA

The construction of these magnificent structures was begun in A.D. 35 by Caligula and completed in 49 by Claudius. The aqueducts were 69 km in length, only 15 km of which were above ground. They carried water from springs in Cerulea and Curtia. They remain isolated in the Compagna Romana (which can be reached by taking the Via Tuscolana southeast, turning south on Via Quadraro, and then west on Viccolo Aquadetto Felice). An early morning or late afternoon walk through these ruins is among the most inspiring and memorable of Rome's experiences.

AQUEDOTTI DELL'ACQUA CLAUDIA

Located just south and west of the Porta Maggiore at the intersection of Via Statilia and Via Eleniana, the Aqueducts of Claudius were begun by Caligula in A.D. 35, completed in 49, restored by Vespasian in 71, and again by Titus in 81. Other sections of the aqueducts continue behind the buildings on the left. The portion in the photograph corresponds to the right hand section in the Piranesi engraving (ca. 1745).

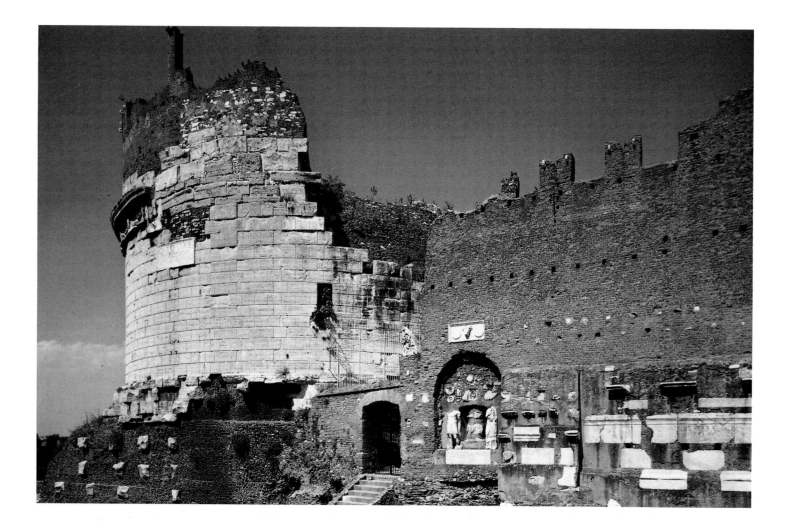

TOMBA DI CECILIA METELLA

Located on the Via Appia, approximately one mile from the Porta S. Sebastiano, this imposing cylindrical tomb was built at the beginning of the Augustan era by Crassus for his wife, Cecilia Metella. In the fourteenth century, the Caetani family turned the tomb into a keep, incorporating it into the adjacent fortress and adding the crenellations. The wall of the fortress to the right of the tomb contains fragments of other tombs from the Via Appia. Piranesi engraving, 1763.

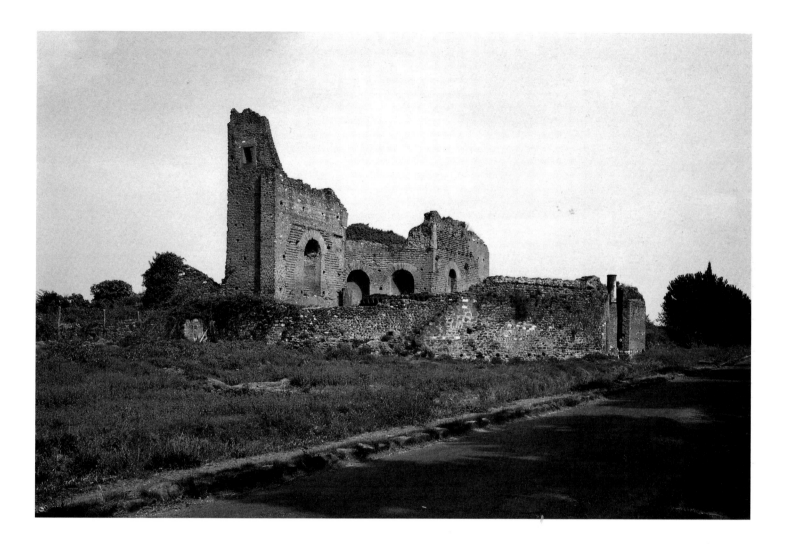

VILLA DEI QUINTILI I

The ruins of the Villa of the Quintilii, along the Via Appia, were so extensive—almost the size of a township—that they were referred to as Roma Vecchia. The villa dates from the time of Hadrian (117–138). Lead pipes inscribed with the family name indicate it belonged to the Quintili brothers. Wealthy and influential, they were nonetheless put to death by Commodus, who coveted their possessions. The villa remained intact until about the fourth century.

CASAL ROTONDO

Located on the Via Appia, approximately 8 km from the Porta S. Sebastiano, this unusual tomb, which has a house and an olive grove above it, dates from the Republican era. It is approximately 36 meters in diameter and is believed to have been built in honor of the poet Messala Corvinus by his son Valerius Maximus Cotta. Curiously, the title of the 1750 Piranesi engraving reads *Sepolcro de Famiglia de' Scipioni;* the actual Tombs of the Scipioni Family are located not on the Via Appia but rather on the Via Porta S. Sebastiano, north of the Porta S. Sebastiano.

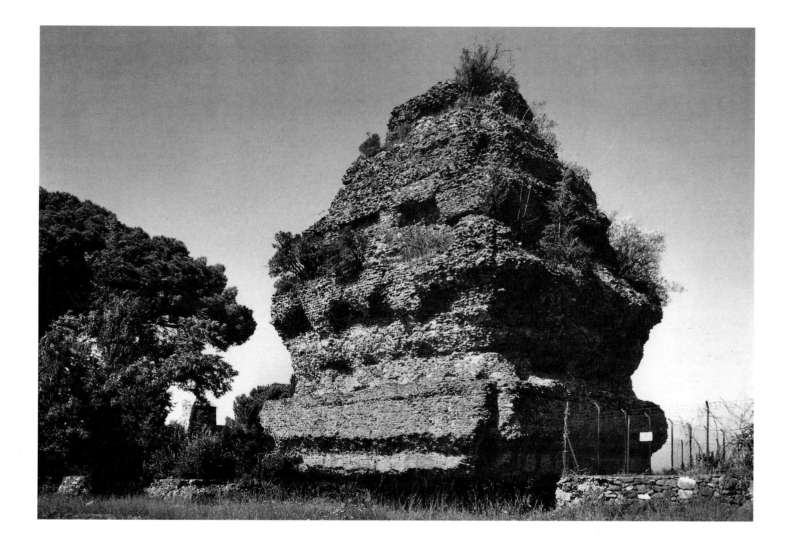

TOMBA GRANDE

Burials within the city were forbidden by laws that date as far back as the fifth century B.C. Located about five miles from Porta S. Sebastiano are the remains of the Tomb of the Metelli, sometimes referred to as the Tomba Grande. Piranesi engraving, ca. 1756.

TOMBA DI "NERO"

This tomb is located on the ancient Via Cassia, five miles from the Porta del Popolo. It is believed to be the second-century tomb of Vibius Maranus. Piranesi engraving, ca. 1756.

GROTTA DELLA NINFA EGERIA

This enchanting grotto is carved into the side of a hill overlooking the Valley of the Caffarella. It can be found at the end of an overgrown and winding path leading down from the Church of S. Urbano. Confusion about its name derives from a legend that the grotto was the setting for the union of Numa, second king of Rome, and Egeria, the Roman goddess of water. Their union symbolized the legitimacy of Rome. The grotto is believed to be a second-century nymphaeum dedicated to Almo, the nymph of the nearby brook, and part of an estate built by Herodes Atticus. The Piranesi engraving (ca. 1766) depicts not just the grotto, but S. Urbano as well. In fact, S. Urbano is located beyond this view of the grotto.

TEMPIO DELLA SALUTE

This remote temple (also referred to as the Temple of Salus), was built in the second century A.D. It is located near the intersection of the Via Appia Nuova and the Via Bisignano, just past the intersection of the Via Appia and the Via Appia Pignatelli. The view is of the northwest and southeast elevations. Piranesi engraving, 1763.

TEMPIO DEL DIO REDICULO

Approximately 100 meters from the church of Domine Quo Vadis on the Via Appia is the the Via della Caffarella. Approximately 0.8 km further along this road is the Temple of the Deus Rediculus, occasionally called the Temple of the Camenae. This small building, now on private land, is visible from the roadside. Remarkably well preserved, much of the terra-cotta detailing is intact or restored. Some scholars believe it was built in the mid-second century as a tomb for Annia Regilia, the wife of Herodes Atticus. The 1773 Piranesi engraving indicates the presence of the nearby Grotto of Egeria (p. 89) and S. Urbano (p. 116), which are not visible from this site.

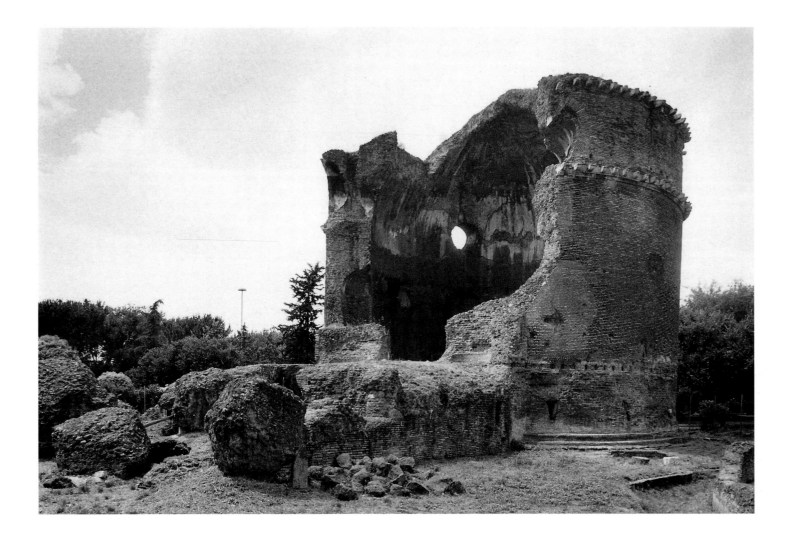

VILLA DEI GORDIANI, TEMPIO

The third-century Villa of the Gordians is located on the Via Prenestina, 2.5 miles from the Porta Maggiore. The villa contained a portico of 200 columns, a basilica, baths, a nymphaeum, and this temple, also known as the Tor de' Schiavi.

VILLA DEI GORDIANI, NINFEO

The exact function of the villa's large octagonal hall is not known. Some believe it may have been
part of a nymphaeum in the vast complex. During the Middle Ages, the villa was used as a fortress.

NINFEO DORICO

Grottos (nymphaea) dedicated to the water gods are found in the Alban Hills outside of Rome. The Grotto of Dorico may date as early as the Republican era. Piranesi engraving, ca. 1762.

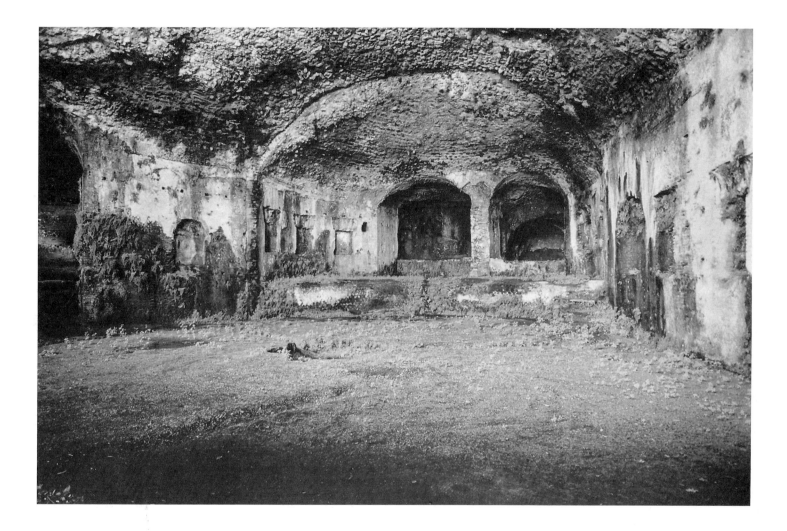

GROTTA DEL BERGANTINO

One of two very sizable nymphaea carved into the side of the Alban Hills, the Grotto of Bergantino is thought to date from the Republican era. Though eroded even in Piranesi's time (engraving, ca. 1762), it is still possible to sense their mystery and drama.

VILLA SETTE BASSI, ENTRANCE

The ruins of the Villa Sette Bassi are located off the Via Tuscolana (a branch of the ancient Via Latina), just beyond Cinecittà on the Via delle Campannelle. This seldom-visited site, in an area called the Roma Vecchia, dates from the time of Domitian (A.D. 81–96). The Piranesi engraving (ca. 1766) depicts the remaining supports of an architecturally innovative cryptoporticus over 300 meters in length. Reconstructions of the complex suggest that the gateway depicted in the foreground was at the northwest corner of the garden. The photograph shows the remains of the southeast section of the cryptoporticus.

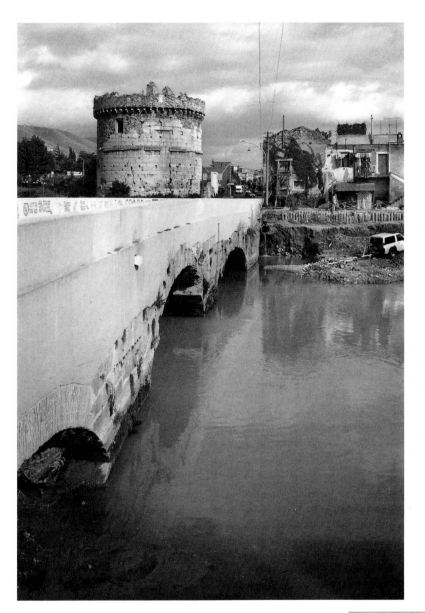

PONTE LUCANO, TOMBE DEI PLAUZI

The ancient bridge over the Aniene in Tivoli, named for Lucanus Plautius, was destroyed by the Goths and rebuilt by Narses. It was again rebuilt several times between the fifteenth century and the nineteenth century. The round Tomb of the Plautii dates from the Augustan era, first century A.D., and resembles the Tomb of Cecilia Metella (p. 84). Piranesi engraving, 1763.

TEMPIO DELLA SIBILLA, TIVOLI

This circular temple, now thought to be a Temple of Vesta, is similar to the one in Rome (p. 51). It dates from the last years of the Republic and was converted into the Church of S. Maria della Rotonda in the Middle Ages. Ten Corinthian columns survive from the original eighteen. To the immediate right is the small building used as the Church of S. Giorgio until 1884. This structure may be the actual Temple of the Sibyl. The view is of the northeast quadrant. Piranesi engraving, 1761.

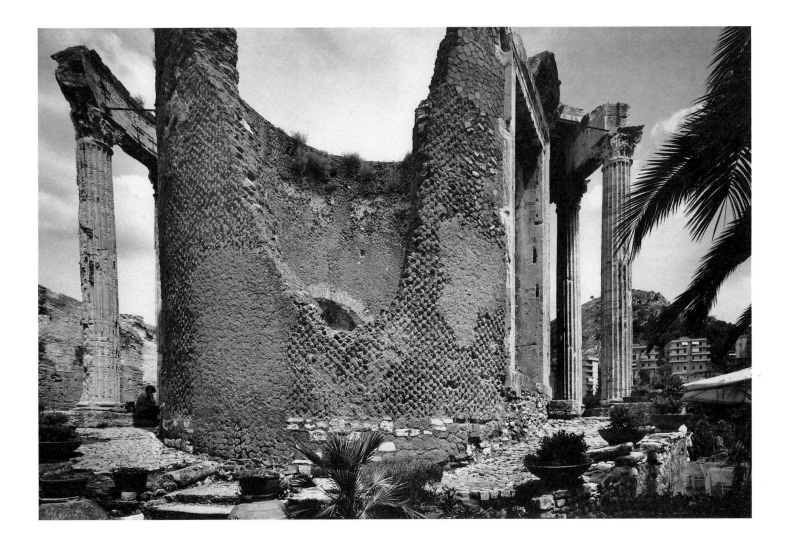

TEMPIO DELLA SIBILLA, TIVOLI

The Ristorante Sibilla now stands on the grounds of the ancient temple. Piranesi engraving, 1761.

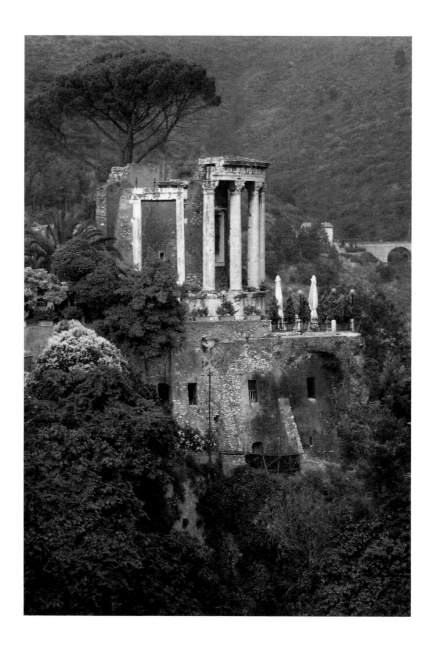

TEMPIO DELLA SIBILLA, TIVOLI

This view of the temple depicts the southeast quadrant that faces the waterfalls. The arches of the substructure seen in the 1761 Piranesi engraving have been filled in.

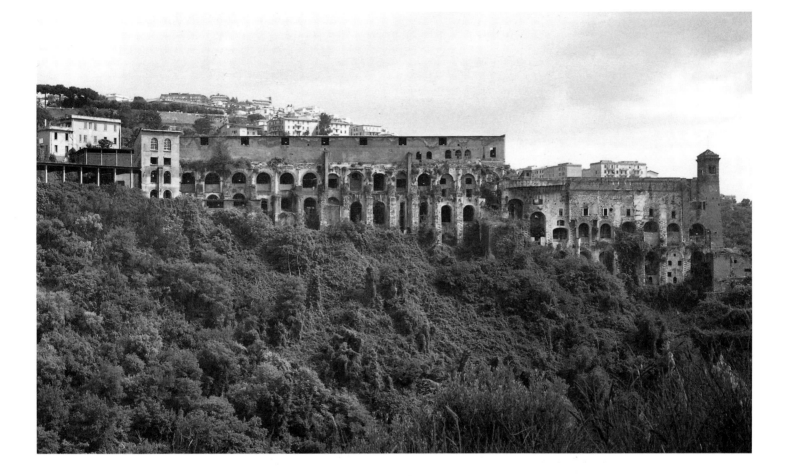

TEMPIO DI ERCOLE VINCITORE, TIVOLI

This Hellenistic sanctuary, also called the Temple of Hercules Victor, is believed to date either from the last half of the first century B.C. or the second century B.C. It was considered to be the most important sanctuary in the city. The old road to Tivoli passed through the vaults in the base. Until recently it was an abandoned paper mill, but it is now being excavated. The photograph looks across the Aniene Valley to the facade facing northwest. The vantage point of the 1763 Piranesi engraving is now completely inaccessible.

TEMPIO DELLA TOSSE, TIVOLI

Located in a private vineyard off the Via delle Cascatelle, near the Temple of Hercules Victor, this small fourth-century temple is very difficult to find, even with a map. The exterior is circular in form; the interior, octagonal. Traces of Byzantine decoration suggest that it may have been a small church. It is also thought to have been a tomb for the Turcia Family. Piranesi engraving, 1763.

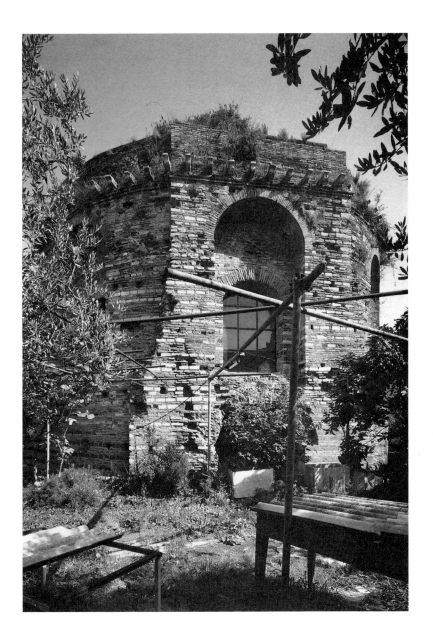

TEMPIO DELLA TOSSE, TIVOLI

Access to the interior of the temple is forbidden because of structural instability.

VILLA ADRIANA, PECILE

Hadrian became emperor in 117 after Trajan's death. His villa, begun around 118, was the largest imperial villa in the Roman Empire and entirely of his own design. Many of the buildings were inspired by classical monuments he visited. The *stoa poekile* ("painted porch"), for example, was an Athenian building associated with the Stoic philosophers. Hadrian's reproduction was 232 x 97 meters. The remaining 9-meter-high north wall is one of the last examples of the diaper-pattern latticework technique formed by setting blocks of tufa on their edge. The view is to the east in the direction of the Hall of the Philosophers (p. 107). Piranesi engraving, 1770.

VILLA ADRIANA, TERME GRANDE

The Great Baths had a circular hall, skylights, and extensive vaulting. This view, facing north, is from a position further into the central room from that of the 1770 Piranesi engraving.

VILLA ADRIANA, TERME PICCOLE

Located in the Small Baths adjacent to a rectangular hall (possibly the frigidarium), this domed space might have served as a changing room. It has harmonious proportions and alternating curved and straight sides that are repeated inside the vault. Piranesi engraving, 1777.

VILLA ADRIANA, SALA DEI FILOSOFI

The Hall of the Philosophers is believed to have been a reading room with an apse and seven niches for bookcases. Piranesi's 1774 engraving alters the proportions of the room by foreshortening the left-hand wall.

VILLA ADRIANA, CANOPO

Hadrian built the Canopus to remind him of the Egyptian town of Canope with its Sanctuary of Serapis. The statuary-lined canal leading to the Canopus recalls the road from Alexandria to Canope with its temple and garden-lined canal.

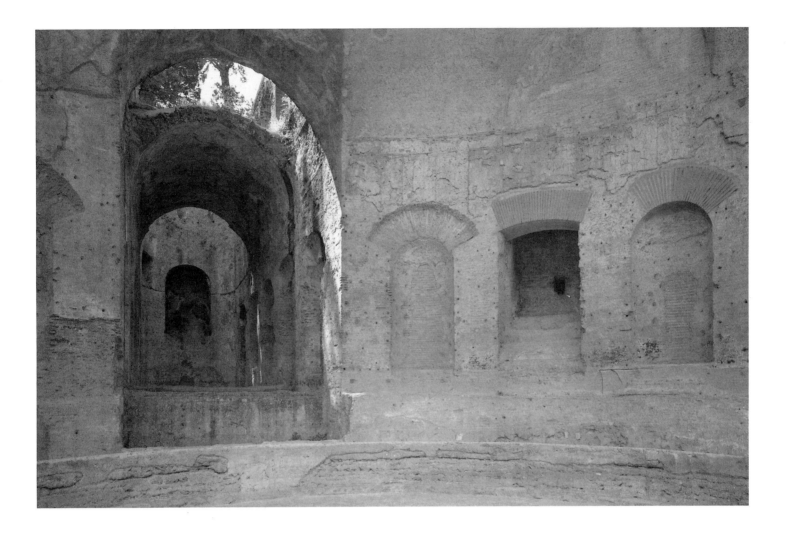

VILLA ADRIANA, CANOPO, INTERIOR

The hemicycle at the south end of the Canal of the Canopus is also known as the Serapheum. The nymphaeum was thought to honor Neptune. The three niches on the right are part of the exterior curve. The corridor, seen at the left, has a fountain at the end flanked by ten niches that held statuary. Most of the Egyptian statues now in the Capitoline and Vatican museums were found here. Piranesi engraving, 1776.

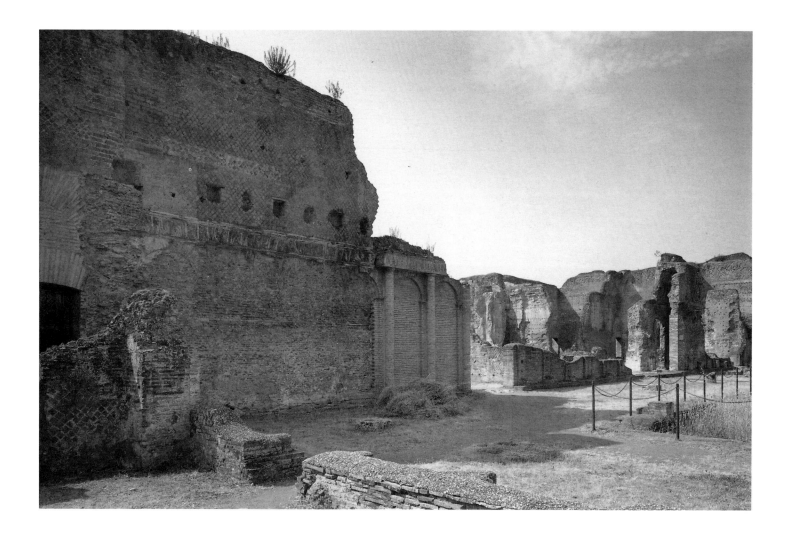

VILLA ADRIANA, PIAZZA D'ORO

Located at the southeast end of the Imperial Palace, the Piazza d'Oro was so named because excavations in the area produced great treasure. This view depicts the southeast wall, looking into the rectangular space. Piranesi's 1776 engraving "pulls" the wall back for a better view of the interior.

VILLA ADRIANA, HELIOCAMINO

Piranesi believed that the openings in the vault were designed to heat this underground room. Hence, his designation "heliocaminus." It is now believed that the orientation of the windows provided only illumination. Piranesi engraving, 1777.

CHIESA NUOVA

CHRISTIAN ROME

S. MARTINO AI MONTI

S. Sylvester I of Mount Soracte founded a church on this site in the fourth century. S. Symmachus replaced it with a Carmelite church around 500 and dedicated it to S. Sylvester and S. Martin. To the right of the apse is the medieval Torre dei Capocci that leads to S. Prassede.

114

S. COSTANZA

S. Costanza is located next to the church of Sant'Agnese, off the Via Nomentana. It was built around 354 by Constantina as a mausoleum for herself and her sister, Helene, and consecrated as a church in 1254. The interior has an annular vault with 24 paired granite columns with Corinthian capitals that support the 22.5-meter dome. The mosaics in the vault date from the fourth century; those on the side niches are thought to be from the fifth or seventh century. The church is best seen in early morning light. Piranesi engraving, ca. 1749–1750.

S. URBANO

S. Urbano was originally a temple in the second-century villa of Herodes Atticus, the wealthy arts patron and the Greek language tutor of Marcus Aurelius. It was converted into a church in the eighth century. When it was restored by Urban VIII in 1634, four fluted columns were incorporated into the wall for structural reinforcement. Located off the Via Appia Pignatelli near the Grotto of Egeria (p. 89), it is now a popular location for weddings. Piranesi uses the church as a landmark in his engravings of neighboring buildings. Piranesi engraving, 1756–1757.

S. URBANO, INTERIOR

The eleventh-century frescoes by Bonizzo depict the life of S. Urbano. The 1767 engraving by Piranesi greatly elongates the nave and does not convey the true intimacy of the church.

S. CRISOGONO, TRASTEVERE

Archaeologists found traces of this fifth-century building six meters beneath the current floor level. The church was altered by Gregory III in the eighth century and finally abandoned in the twelfth century. The present structure, next to a bus depot on the busy Viale Trastevere, was begun in 1123 by John of Crema and reconstructed in 1623 by G. B. Soria under the patronage of Cardinal Scipione Borghese. The last major restoration took place in 1866. The campanile was built in the twelfth century; the spire was added in the sixteenth century. Vasi engraving, 1756.

S. CECILIA IN TRASTEVERE

S. Cecilia, the patron saint of music, is said to have invented the organ. She was martyred in 230.
The first basilica on this site was built during the reign of Paschal I (817–824). S. Cecilia's remains
were transferred from the Catacombs of S. Calisto in 820. The church was severely modified in the
sixteenth century, but was partly restored to its original form in 1899. The campanile dates from
around 1120. Vasi engraving, 1758.

S. MARIA IN COSMEDIN

This medieval Roman church incorporates two earlier buildings: the arcaded colonnade was part of the Imperial Market Inspector's office; the side walls were part of an early Christian welfare center that had an oratory. Hadrian I enlarged the church in the eighth century, and it later became a Greek church. The name "in Cosmedin" may refer to the decorative style of this era. The church was rebuilt in the twelfth century; the porch and campanile were added by Calixtus II. The famous "Boca della Verita," the Mouth of Truth, is located on this porch. The eighteenth-century facade was demolished in 1894. Vasi engraving, 1753.

S. NICOLA IN CARCERE

This eleventh-century church was consecrated in 1128. It occupies the site of three Republican-era temples in the Forum Holitorium; the side walls incorporate columns from two of these temples. The name "in Carcere" refers to the Byzantine jail that occupied one of the temples in 7 B.C. The present facade was designed by Giacomo della Porta in 1599. The medieval tower dates from the twelfth century when the Perleone family controlled this district. The photograph depicts the east (primary) and north facade. Although the 1756 Vasi engraving also depicts the east facade, it does not include the tower.

S. BARTOLOMEO

Located on Tiber Island, S. Bartolomeo was built in the tenth century in honor of S. Adalbert, the Bishop of Prague. At the far right is the Ponte Rotto, the Broken Bridge. Originally called the Pons Aemelius, it was the first stone bridge built over the Tiber. The original piers date from 179 B.C. and the arches from 142 B.C. The bridge collapsed in 1575, was rebuilt, and collapsed again in 1598. Vasi engraving, ca. 1754–1775.

S. GIORGIO IN VELABRO

This ancient church is located just east of the Arch of Janus (p. 68). The church was built in the ninth century on the site of a seventh-century vestry. The Ionic portico was restored in the twelfth century when the campanile was added. To the left is the Arcus Argentariorum (Arch of the Moneychangers), A.D. 204, which was restored in 1986. The church, which has been a favorite Roman wedding site, was severely damaged in recent bombings. Vasi engraving, 1753.

SS. GIOVANNI E PAOLO

The house of S. Giovanni and S. Paolo is thought to have been located on this site on the Coelian Hill. The church was first established in a private house in the second or third century. After being demolished in the eleventh century, it was rebuilt by Paschal II at the beginning of the twelfth century. The five arches above the porch are part of the original building. The twelfth-century campanile and the convent on the right stand atop the Temple of Claudius (p. 61). At the far left are the arches of third-century Roman shops and the Clivo di Scauro descending beneath the buttresses of the church. Vasi engraving, 1753.

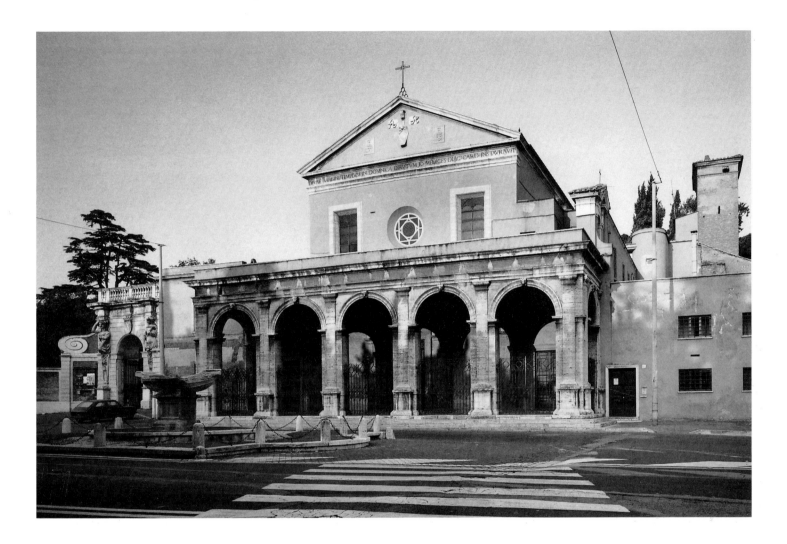

S. MARIA DOMNICA

This church is located on the summit of the Coelian Hill, adjacent to the Arch of Dolabella (p. 77) and the entrance to the Villa Celimontana. It was restored by St. Paschal I (817–824) and rebuilt by Leo X (1513–1521). The porch was added by Andrea Sansovino. It is also called S. Maria della Navicella, referring to the stone boat that Leo X made into a fountain and placed at the front of the church. Vasi engraving, 1753.

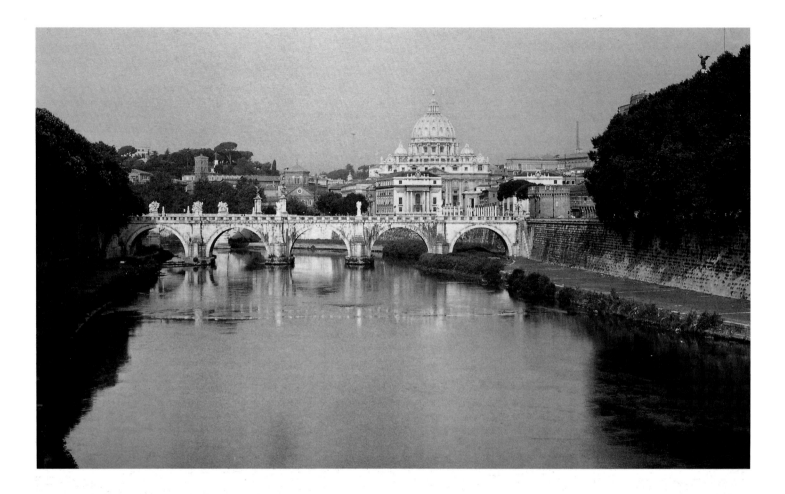

PONTE S. ANGELO E IL DUOMO DI S. PIETRO

This view, looking west to St. Peter's and the Castel S. Angelo, is one of the most popular depictions of Rome. The Ponte S. Angelo (originally the Pons Aelius or Pons Adrianus) was built by Hadrian in A.D. 134. Subsequent additions include the statues of St. Peter and St. Paul by Clement VII in 1530 and ten statues of angels designed by Bernini in 1688. Piranesi engraving, 1750–1751.

PIAZZA S. PIETRO

This world-famous piazza, built between 1656 and 1667, is a masterpiece of civic architecture. Bernini's brilliant plan for Alexander VII featured two semicircular colonnades representing the open arms of the church and creating an embracing approach to the great basilica. Each colonnade has a quadruple row of Doric columns, 284 in all. The broad, low colonnade was designed to minimize the width of the basilica and accentuate its height. The 350-ton granite obelisk was carved in the first century B.C., brought to Rome in A.D. 37 by Caligula, and erected in the piazza in 1567 by Sixtus V. The east facade of the basilica was designed by Carlo Maderno in 1607–1614. Piranesi engraving, 1772.

S. PIETRO, INTERIOR

The largest of all Christian sanctuaries, St. Peter's is 186 meters long, 137 meters wide across the transepts, and is crowned by Michelangelo's great dome, measuring 42 meters in diameter. It has 500 columns, 450 statues, and 50 altars. The construction of St. Peter's spanned 120 years and the reigns of 20 popes, from Julius II and his architects Bramante and da Sangallo, to Urban VIII and his favorite architect, Bernini. Standing above the space believed to be the tomb of St. Peter is the High Altar. Over this rises the 29-meter baroque Baldacchino designed by Bernini and unveiled by Urban VIII in 1633, which is cast of bronze removed from the Pantheon. In the 1773 Piranesi engraving, the arches of the transept appear on either side of the Baldacchino. In the photograph, the arches are those of the crossing immediately east of the transept.

S. MARIA MAGGIORE, EAST FACADE

According to a thirteenth-century legend, the Virgin Mary appeared to Pope Liberius in the summer of 352, and instructed him to build a church on the Esquiline Hill, on the spot which would be indicated the following morning by a patch of snow. Thus, the original name, S. Maria della Neve (snow). One of four patriarchal basilicas, S. Maria Maggiore is thought to date from the fifth century, completed by Sixtus III (423–440). The east facade was designed by Fuga in 1743. The campanile, the tallest in Rome, was given its present design in 1377 by Gregory XI. The 14.5-meter cipollino column was crowned with a statue of the Virgin Mary and placed in the square in 1613 for Paul V by Carlo Maderno who also designed the fountain. Piranesi engraving, ca.1746–1748.

S. MARIA MAGGIORE, INTERIOR

This basilica has undergone numerous restorations and changes since it was built by Sixtus III in 423. The vast interior (86 meters long) is divided into a nave and aisles by 36 Ionic columns, arranged by Ferdinando Fuga for Benedict XIV in 1743–1750. Fuga also added the baldacchino and rebuilt the floor. The coffered ceiling, attributed to Giuliano da Sangallo, is gilded with the first cache of gold brought from Peru for Alexander VI (1492–1503). In the 1768 engraving, Piranesi diminishes the size of human figures to exaggerate the monumentality of the interior.

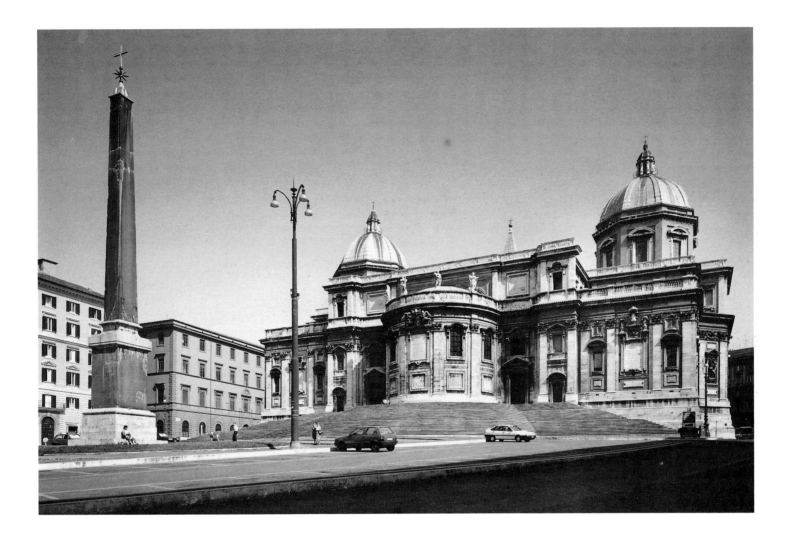

S. MARIA MAGGIORE, WEST FACADE

The apsidal (west) facade that faces the Piazza dell'Esquilino was completed in 1673. The right-hand section and its dome were designed by Flaminio Ponzio. The central and left sections were designed by Carlo Rainaldi, whose conservative schemes were preferred over the elaborate designs of Bernini. The left-hand dome was designed by Domenico Fontana. The Egyptian Obelisk was brought to this site from the Mausoleum of Augustus. Piranesi engraving, 1756–1757.

S. GIOVANNI IN LATERANO, EAST FACADE

S. Giovanni in Laterano, one of Rome's seven great pilgrimage churches, is the actual Cathedral of Rome, and its bishop is the Pope. The church was founded in about 313 by Constantine the Great on the property of the Plauti Laterani, a wealthy Roman family. The present facade was completed in 1734 by Alessandro Galilei. The Lateran Palace, also dating from the time of Constantine, was partially destroyed by fire in 1308. It was rebuilt in 1586. At the far right is the Scala Santa, believed to be the staircase of Pilate's house that Christ descended after his condemnation. Piranesi engraving, ca. 1746–1748.

S. GIOVANNI IN LATERANO, INTERIOR

The interior of this basilica is 130 meters long with two aisles on either side of the nave. In 1650, Innocent X commissioned Borromini to renovate the interior and save it from collapse. He created large recesses in the pillars of the nave to receive the Sculptures of the Apostles designed by Bernini's followers. The ceiling was begun by Pius IV in 1562 following designs of Michelangelo's students. At the end of the nave is the fourteenth-century baldacchino, designed by di Stefano and containing relics of the heads of Saints Peter and Paul and St. Peter's wooden altar table. Piranesi engraving, 1768.

PIAZZA DI S. GIOVANNI IN LATERANO

From left to right are the Lateran Palace, the Egyptian Obelisk (p. 135), S. Giovanni in Laterano (p. 132), and the Baptistry of S. Giovanni. The octagonal Baptistry was built by Constantine in about 314. It was rebuilt in the fifth century by Sixtus III, who added eight porphyry columns to the interior, and again in 884 by Hadrian III. Its design has often been copied for other baptistries. Piranesi engraving, 1775.

OBELISCO EGIZIO

The "Lateranensis," the tallest obelisk in Rome (32 meters), was created for the Temple of Ammon in Thebes in the fifteenth century B.C. Constantine II moved the obelisk to Rome in 357 and placed it in the Circus Maximus. There it eventually toppled and remained hidden until it was rediscovered by Fontana in 1587. Sixtus V ordered it placed in its present location in the Piazza di S. Giovanni in Laterano. To the right is the Lateran Palace. Piranesi engraving, ca.1749–1750.

S. PAOLO FUORI LE MURA

According to tradition, the body of St. Paul was buried in a vineyard on this site. One of the four patriarchal basilicas and the largest church in Rome after St. Peter's, this nineteenth-century reconstruction is the third one built on this site. The first shrine was built around 384 and was subsequently enlarged. After being pillaged in the ninth century, it was restored in 1070 by Gregory VII. In 1823, the basilica was virtually destroyed by fire. The present structure was begun by Leo XII in 1823. The transept was consecrated in 1840 and the church in 1854 by Pius IX. Both the photograph and the Piranesi engraving (ca.1757–1758) depict the west facade.

S. PAOLO FUORI LE MURA

The nineteenth-century reconstruction, begun after the fire of 1823, followed the original Egyptian cross plan. Eighty granite columns divide the nave and four aisles. The triumphal arch, supported by two granite columns, is a relic from the old basilica. The ceiling bears the arms of Pius IX (1846–1878) who consecrated the church. In his engraving (ca. 1748–1748) Piranesi cuts a section through the left arcade, a graphic device he employed only this once.

S. SEBASTIANO FUORI LE MURA

S. Sebastiano, one of the seven pilgrimage churches, is located outside the walls of Rome on the Via Appia. It was originally dedicated to Saints Peter and Paul, whose bodies were temporarily moved here during the persecution of Valerian in 258. The first church, built in the fourth century, was a covered cemetery over the extensive catacombs. In the ninth century it was renamed for S. Sebastiano. Flaminio Ponzio rebuilt the church in 1609–1612 for Cardinal Scipio Borghese. Piranesi engraving, 1761.

S. LORENZO FUORI LE MURA

S. Lorenzo is one of the seven pilgrimage churches. Constantine built a sanctuary on this site in 330 for pilgrims to the tomb of S. Lorenzo. It was rebuilt by Pelagius II in 579 and enlarged in the eighth century. Between 1216 and 1227, Honorius II extended the nave, reversed its orientation, demolished the apses and thus joined the thirteenth- and sixth-century buildings. The Romanesque bell tower dates from the twelfth century. In 1943, a bomb destroyed the roof, the porch, and part of the walls. Subsequent repairs attempted to restore its thirteenth-century design. The statue of S. Lorenzo atop the column was designed in 1865 by Galletti. Piranesi engraving, 1760–1761.

S. MARIA IN TRASTEVERE

Pope Calixtus built the first sanctuary on this site in 217, marking the Miracle of the Fountain of Oil (38 B.C.). The first full-sized basilica, built by Julius II (337–352), was altered in the ninth century by Gregory IV. The present-day basilica was built in 1140 by Innocent II during his tumultuous reign. The church was subsequently altered through the nineteenth century. The elaborate mosaic of the Virgin and Child with the accompanying procession of women dates from the twelfth or thirteenth century. The statues of the saints were added in the seventeenth century, and the porch was restored in the eighteenth century. The fountain at the far right was redesigned by Bernini in 1659. Vasi engraving, 1753.

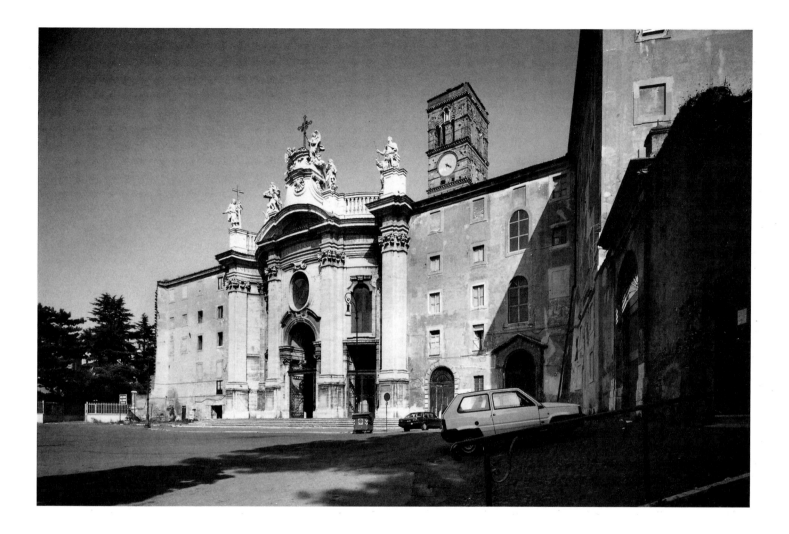

S. CROCE IN GERUSALEMME

Constantine's mother, St. Helen, brought back a relic of the true cross from her pilgrimage to Jerusalem in 329. Her home, the Palatium Sessorium, stood on this site. In her memory, Constantine converted part of the palace into a church by adding an apse to the palace atrium. It is one of the seven pilgrimage churches of Rome and has been occupied by Cistercians since 1561. It was rebuilt in 1144 by Lucius II, who added the campanile, and was modernized in 1743 by Benedict XIV, who added the unusual oval vestibule. On the far right is a portion of the Anfiteatro Castrense (p. 52). Piranesi engraving, 1757–1758.

TERME DI DIOCLEZIANO, S. MARIA DEGLI ANGELI

The Baths of Diocletian, built between 295 and 305, were the largest and most beautiful of the over 900 bathhouses in Rome. They were abandoned in 538. In 1561, Pius IV commissioned the 86- year-old Michelangelo to convert the ruins into a church. After years of dissociated alterations to the plan, Vanvitelli was asked to unify the effort in 1749. Unfortunately, he altered Michelangelo's orientation and placed the entrance on this southwest elevation. His outer facade was destroyed in the early twentieth century, leaving only the doorway. Piranesi engraving, 1774.

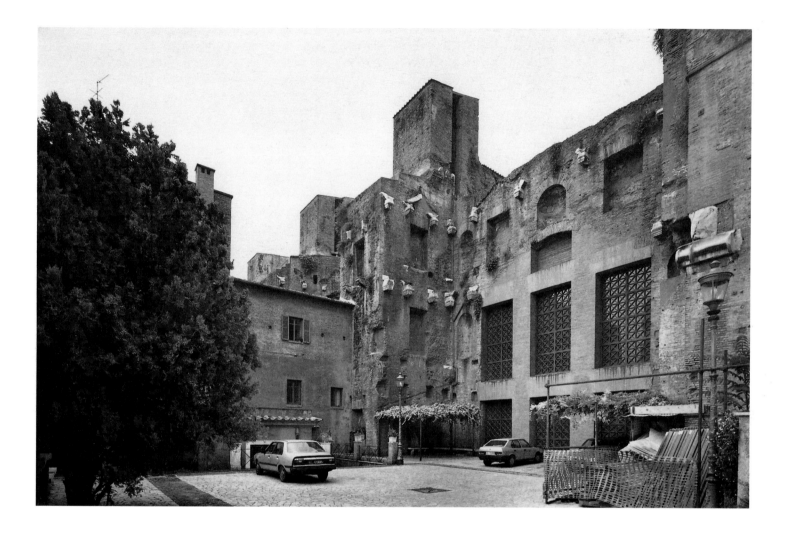

TERME DI DIOCLEZIANO, NORTH WALL

This view of the north wall of the remaining ruins is actually the south wall of the Frigidarium.
This wall was not incorporated into Michelangelo's designs for converting the baths into the
church of S. Maria degli Angeli (p. 144). Piranesi's 1774 engraving from the northeast eliminates
the additions. The photograph is taken from the northwest.

S. MARIA DEGLI ANGELI

S. Maria degli Angeli occupies the central hall of the Baths of Diocletian. The conversion, designed by Michelangelo between 1563 and 1566 for Pius I, placed the entrance on the southeast corner, creating a nave of vast proportions. Vanvitelli relocated the entrance in 1749, destroying the effect and turning the nave into a transept. To create his new apse and chancel, he pushed through the southwest wall of the frigidarium (p. 143). This view is from the southeast corner, showing the west vestibule wall (the tepidarium) on the left and the east transept on the right. To create his 1776 view, Piranesi "removed" part of the wall.

S. MARIA DEL ORTO

S. Maria del Orto was built in 1566 by Guidetto Guidetti under the patronage of the Università degli Ortolani (Greengrocers). The facade is attributed to Vignola and was finished by Francesco da Volterra.

TRINITÀ DEI MONTI

The Piazza della Trinità dei Monti is located at the top of the Spanish Steps (p. 167). The church of Trinità dei Monti was begun in 1493 by Louis XII. The double stairway was built in 1587 by Domenico Fontana, and the clock was added in 1613. After the destruction by Napoleon, the church was restored in 1816. The obelisk was erected in 1788.

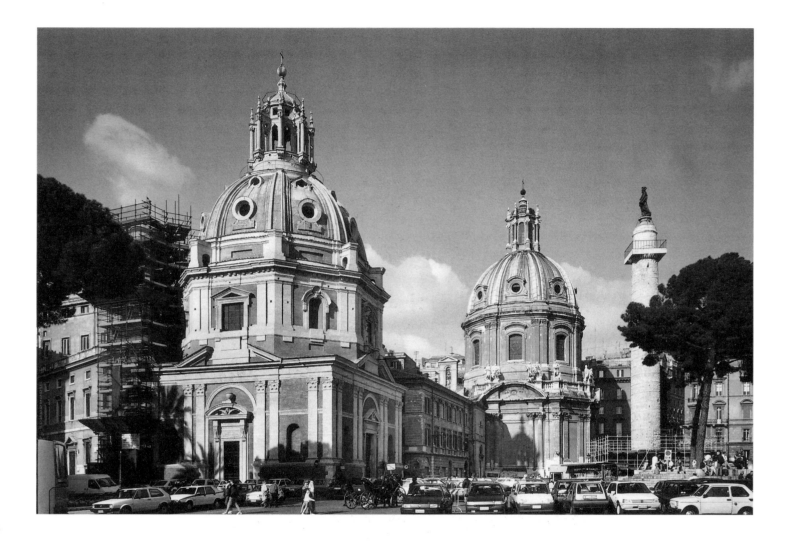

S. MARIA LORETO E SS. NOME DI MARIA

These domed churches, similar in design, stand at the western end of the Via Fori Imperiali. S. Maria Loreto (on the left) was begun by Antonio da Sangallo in 1502 and completed by Michelangelo's pupil, Giacomo del Duca, between 1525 and 1577. SS. Nome di Maria was built by Antoine Derizet between 1736 and 1741. To the right of the churches is the Column of Trajan (p. 58). Both the photograph and 1763 Piranesi engraving look northeast from the area now occupied by the Vittorio Emanuele II Monument.

S. MARIA DELLA PACE

Located northwest of the Piazza Navona, S. Maria della Pace was rebuilt by Sixtus IV (1480–1484) to celebrate his victory over the Turks. Baccio Pontelli is thought to have been the architect. It was partially rebuilt in 1611. Alexander VII (1655–1667) chose Pietro da Cortona to design the facade and semicircular porch with its Tuscan columns. The interior contains Raphael's Sibyls, a chapel by Antonio da Sangallo the Younger, portions of frescoes by Rosso Fiorentino, a high altar by Carlo Maderno, and cloisters by Bramante. Vasi engraving, 1756.

S. ANDREA DELLA VALLE

S. Andrea della Valle was begun in 1591 by Fra Fr. Grimaldi and continued by Carlo Maderno.
The facade was built between 1655 and 1665 by Carlo Rainaldi. Piranesi engraving, ca. 1745.

S. GREGORIO MAGNO

S. Gregory the Great founded a monastery on this site at the end of the sixth century and dedicated it to S. Andrew. It was rededicated to St. Gregory the Great in the twelfth century. Except for two chapels, it was demolished in 1573. G. B. Soria began the restoration in 1633, under the patronage of Cardinal Scipione Borghese.

S. CATERINA DEI FUNARI

The facade of S. Caterina dei Funari was designed by Giudetto Giudetti in 1564 and restored in 1978. The shallow pilasters are Renaissance in style, whereas the decorative garlands are elements typical of the Counter-Reformation.

SS. DOMENICO E SISTO

SS. Domenico e Sisto was built under the successive direction of Giacomo della Porta, Nicola and Orazio Torriani, and Vincenzo della Greco. It was completed in 1655. The grand staircase leading to the church was designed by della Greco. The church marks the beginning of Via Panisperna, which runs directly to S. Maria Maggiore.

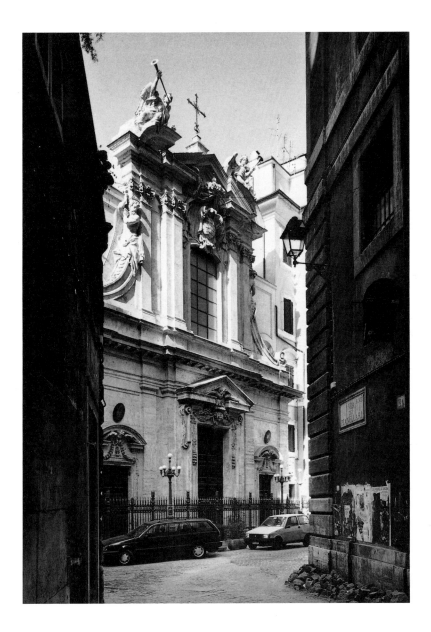

S. ANTONIO DEI PORTUGHESE

S. Antonio dei Portughese, the national church of Portugal, is located off the Via della Scrofa on Via dei Portughesi. It was begun in the seventeenth century by Martino Longhi the Younger, continued by Carlo Rainaldi, and completed by Cristoforo Schor in 1695. It features a rococo facade and, at its pinnacle, angels blowing stone trumpets toward the medieval Torre della Scimmia (p. 179). Both the church and the tower are celebrated in Hawthorne's *The Marble Faun*.

S. PIETRO IN VINCOLI

In 439, the Empress Eudoxia, wife of Theodosius the Younger, was presented with the two chains that bound St. Peter at Tullianum. In 442, she gave one to her daughter, the wife of Valentinian III, who presented them to S. Leo I. As a shrine, S. Leo I then built the Church of S. Pietro in Vincoli. Sixtus IV restored the church in 1475. Meo del Caprina designed the facade with its colonnaded portico. Vasi engraving, 1753.

CAPPELLA DI "CENCI"

This boarded-up chapel stands in a small square around the corner from the Palazzo Cenci. The chapel is said by some to contain the bodies of Giacomo Cenci and his sister, Beatrice, beheaded in 1599 for suspected patricide. However, she is believed to be buried in S. Pietro in Montorio.

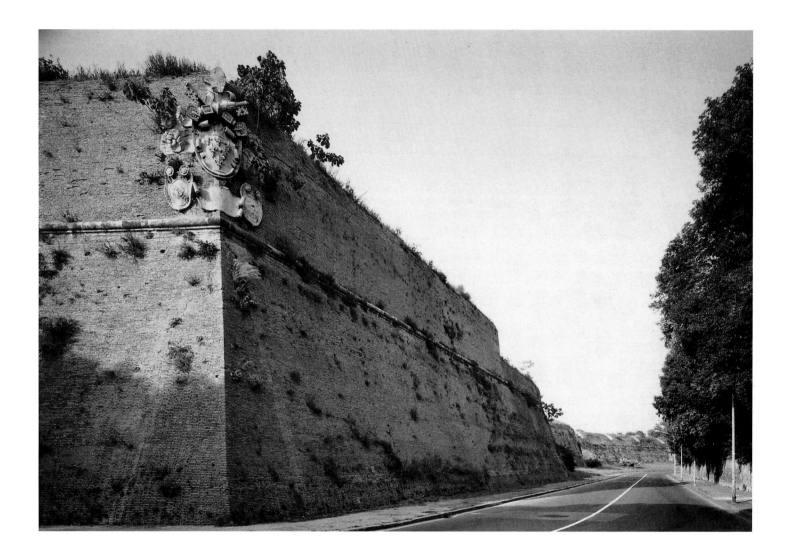

BASTIONE DEL SANGALLO

In 1537, Paul III held a competition for the design of the fortifications between the Porta S. Sebastiano and the Porta S. Paolo. Antonio da Sangallo the Younger won the competition, and his bastions are now considered a model of military architecture. The Farnese family *stemma* (coat of arms) of Paul III appears at the corner. Rossini engraving, 1829.

PORTA S. SPIRITO

Leo IV built the Porta S. Spirito in the ninth century. It is named for the adjacent church. In 1540, Paul III had Antonio da Sangallo construct bastions and restore the gate. Though he never finished the work, the gate is often called the Porta del Sangallo. Vasi engraving, 1747.

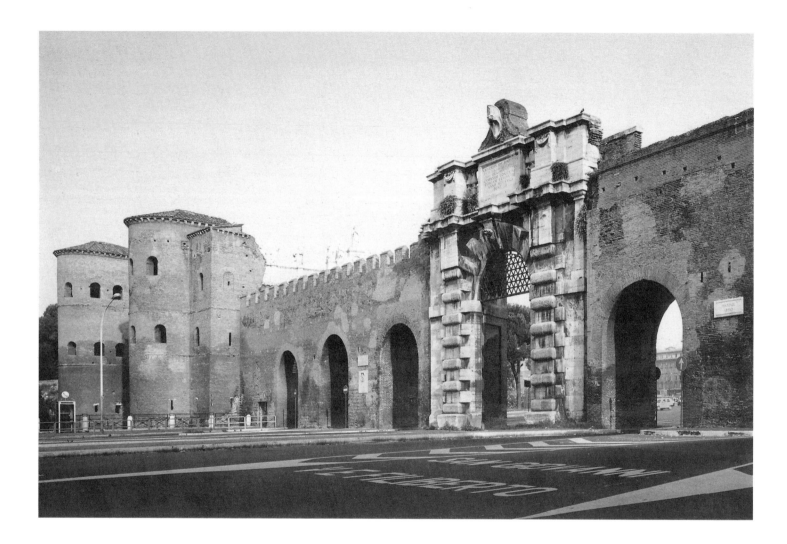

PORTA S. GIOVANNI

The Porta S. Giovanni, located east of S. Giovanni in Laterano (pp. 132–134), was built by
Giaccomo del Duca in 1574 for Gregory XIII. To the left are the towers of the Porta Anisania,
located near the site of the Porta Celimontana of the ancient Servian Wall, 353 B.C. From here the
Via Appia Nuova leads out to the Alban Hills. Both the photograph and the 1747 Vasi engraving
show the south facade from a position outside the wall.

PORTA SETTIMIANA

The Porta Settimiana is located in Trastevere, at the junction of Via Garibaldi and Via della Scala. It was incorporated into the Aurelian Wall and rebuilt by Alexander VI (1492–1503). It marks the beginning of Via della Lungara, the street built by Julius II in 1507 to connect Trastevere with the Borgo. The views are from the Via della Scala, looking at the south facade. Vasi engraving, 1747.

PORTA S. PANCRAZIO

The Porta S. Pancrazio was built by Urban VIII in the early seventeenth century and rebuilt in
1857. Originally called the Porta Aurelia, it marked the beginning of the ancient Via Aurelia,
which led to Etruscan towns west of Rome. It now houses a museum honoring Garibaldi and his
followers, who defended the city from this point.

PORTA PIA

Originally called the Porta Nomentana, the Porta Pia leads to the Via Nomentana, the ancient road to Nomentum. In 1561, Pius IV commissioned Michelangelo (who was over 80 years old at the time) to design the arch for the gate. It was his last completed architectural work. It was struck by lightning in 1851 and later restored by Vespignani for Pius IX. Rossini engraving, 1829.

PORTO DI RIPETTA

The Porto di Ripetta, once a major port, declined in use after 1730 when the silting of the Tiber made navigation impossible. It was demolished in the nineteenth century. S. Girolamo degli Schiavone (Serbs), designed by Longhi the Elder in 1587, still dominates the Via di Ripetta. Piranesi's 1750–1751 engraving depicts the grand stair that led from the dock to the church.

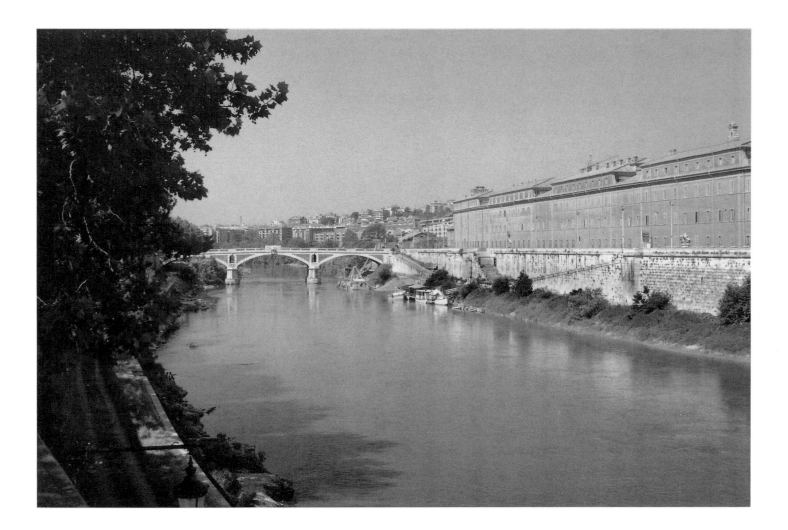

RIPA GRANDE

From ancient times, the Ripa Grande was the major port of Rome. This view to the southwest shows the Istituto di San Michele. It was founded in 1683 as a refuge and training center for homeless children, but is now used for art restoration. The Ponte Aventine was built on the site of the Pons Sublicus, the first bridge across the Tiber. Piranesi engraving, 1757–1758.

PIAZZA NAVONA, VIEW FROM THE SOUTH

The Piazza Navona occupies the site of Domitian's stadium, built in A.D. 86. The stadium was stripped of marble in 356 by Constantinius and was in ruins by the fifth century. Rebuilt in the Renaissance, it was used as a marketplace from 1477 to 1869. In the foreground is the Fountain of the Moor. In 1653, Bernini was commissioned to renovate the fountain and add the central statue of the Moor. At the far left is the Palazzo Pamphilj, completed by Borromini in the mid-sixteenth century. Next to the palazzo is Sant'Agnese in Agone, which was rebuilt in 1652 by Girolamo and Carlo Rainaldi for Innocent X. The concave facade was begun in 1653 by Borromini, who also designed part of the dome. Piranesi engraving, 1773.

PIAZZA NAVONA, VIEW FROM THE NORTH

In the foreground is the Fountain of Neptune, designed by Giacomo della Porta at the end of sixteenth century. The statues were added in 1878. In the midground is the Fountain of the Four Rivers, completed by Bernini in 1651 for Innocent X. The obelisk, from the Domitian era, was found on the Via Appia. On the right are S. Agnese in Agone and the Palazzo Pamphilj. Piranesi engraving, ca. 1746–1748.

PIAZZA DEL POPOLO

This gateway into the city was planned by Pius VI and Pius VII's architect, Giuseppi Valadier (1762–1839). It is named for S. Maria del Popolo, on the far left. This view to the south features the twin churches of S. Maria di Montesanto (left, begun by Rainaldi in 1662 and completed by Bernini in 1675) and S. Maria dei Miracoli (begun by Rainaldi in 1677 and completed by Fontana in 1679). Commissioned by Alexander VII, they create a dramatic entrance to the Via Corso, one of Rome's main arteries. The fourteenth-century B.C. Egyptian obelisk was brought to Rome by Augustus in 30 B.C. and placed here by Sixtus V in 1589. The Piranesi engraving (ca. 1746) distorts the symmetry of the churches to permit a view down the radiating streets.

166

PIAZZA DI SPAGNA

So named in the seventeenth century when the Spanish Ambassador to the Vatican resided here, the Piazza di Spagna has long been the artistic and literary center of Rome. John Keats died in the house immediately to the right of the steps. The grand flight of 137 steps was built between 1721 and 1725 by Fr. De Sanctis to connect the piazza with Trinità dei Monti (p. 146). The photograph, taken at 5:45A.M., depicts a rare moment when the piazza is not inundated with tourists. In his 1750–1751 engraving, Piranesi adopts a high viewpoint and deliberately manipulates the size of the piazza to depict its location relative to the Piazza del Popolo at the far left.

FONTANA DI TREVI

This view from the western corner of the Piazza di Trevi shows Nocola Salvi's eighteenth-century Trevi Fountain in its urban context. To the right is the church of SS. Vicenzo ed Anastasio, which was rebuilt for Cardinal Mazarin in 1630 with the addition of a baroque facade by Martino Longhi the Younger. This view was produced shortly after the major renovation of 1991–1992. Piranesi engraving, ca. 1746–1748.

FONTANA DI TREVI

In 19 B.C., Agrippa built a 20-km canal to bring waters from the Acqua Virginae to his baths. In addition to the Trevi Fountain, these waters also supply the fountains in the Piazza di Spagna, the Piazza Farnese (p. 180), and the Piazza Navona (pp. 164, 165). The original fountain was a simple design by L. B. Alberti. In 1758, Clement X commissioned Nicola Salvi to create a new terminus. His design incorporated a triumphal arch into the entire facade of the Palazzo Poli. In the center, two tritons conduct the chariot of Neptune. Figures of Health (left) and Abundance (right) are in the side niches. Above these are the four seasons; at the top, the Corsini family coat of arms. The 1773 Piranesi engraving exaggerates the size of the surrounding urban fabric.

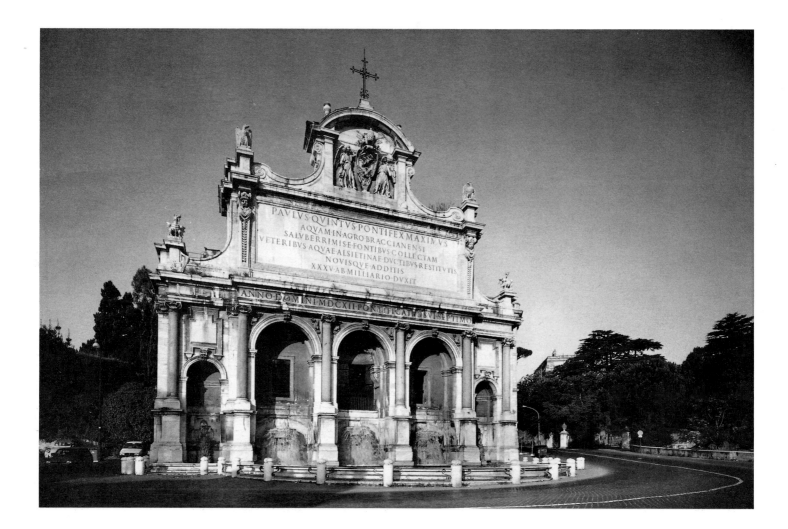

FONTANA DELL'ACQUA PAOLA

In 1612, Paul V commissioned Flaminio Ponzio to design this elaborate fountain high on the Janiculum Hill. The fountain carries water from the ancient Aqueducts of Trajan originating in Lake Bracciano. The design was a variation of the Fontana dell'Acqua Felice (p. 171), but with two additional side bays and without sculpture in the central bays. Marble for the fountain was taken from the Roman Forum and the columns from old St. Peter's. The large basin was designed by Carlo Fontana in 1690. At the right in the 1756–1757 Piranesi engraving is the Villa Aurelia, now part of the American Academy in Rome. The villa's elevated position and visibility from the fountain is highly exaggerated by Piranesi.

FONTANA DELL'ACQUA FELICE

Domenico Fontana was commissioned to design this fountain by Pope Sixtus V (Felice Peretti) in 1585. It was the first "wall fountain" to be built in Rome since ancient times. The statue of Moses in the central bay was designed by Leonardo Sormani in 1588. In the side bays are statues of Aaron by G. della Porta and Gideon by Flaminia Vacca. To the left is the church of S. Maria della Vittoria, designed by Maderno in 1620 with a facade by G. B. Soria. Piranesi "altered" the width of the street to depict the church facade. Piranesi engraving, 1760–1761.

CAMPIDOGLIO

The Capitoline Hill, the smallest of the Seven Hills, has long been the most important and best known. It is the current seat of the Roman administrative offices. At the top left is S. Maria d'Aracoeli, converted from a sixth-century oratory by Franciscan monks in 1250. The steps leading to the church were built in 1346. To the right of the church is a portion of the Palazzo Nuovo, the Capitoline Museum (p. 174). Michelangelo designed La Cordonata, the central stairs leading up to the Piazza del Campidoglio, but the execution was not faithful to his design. In the center is the Palazzo Senatorio. The tower was built in 1578–1582. On the far right is the fifteenth-century Palazzo dei Conservatori. Piranesi engraving, ca. 1746–1748.

CAMPIDOGLIO, TROFEI DI MARIO

This view from northwest of the steps features, among other statuary, one of the Trophies of Marius (second from the left) originally placed atop the Fontana dell'Acqua Giulia (p. 78) in the Middle Ages. In the background is the Palazzo degli Conservatori. Piranesi engraving, 1761.

173

PIAZZA DEL CAMPIDOGLIO

In 1536, Paul III commissioned Michelangelo to redesign this historic center of Rome. His designs, though modified, were carried out over the next hundred years. The resulting Piazza di Campidoglio is among the most beautifully proportioned public spaces in the world. Michelangelo redirected the piazza to face the city rather than the Forum. On the right is the Palazzo Senatorio. Originally a fortress (ca. 1150), Michelangelo's facade design was built between 1582 and 1605. He lived to see only the large double staircase completed. In the center is the Palazzo Nuovo, designed in 1654 by Girolamo and Carlo Rainaldi to match the Palazzo dei Conservatori on the opposite side of the piazza, as per Michelangelo's original plan. Piranesi engraving, 1774.

PIAZZA DEL QUIRINALE

According to legend, the Sabines were the first to settle on this hill. The name Quirinale is derived from their Temple of Quirinus, the name they gave the deified Romulus. From the nearby Baths of Constantine, Sixtus V (1585–1590) brought Roman copies of fifth-century Greek statues. Pius VI placed the obelisk in the piazza in 1786. Pius VII added the basin from the Forum in the early nineteenth century. In the center is the Palazzo del Quirinale and, on the far right, is the Palazzo della Consulta (p. 176). Piranesi's engraving (ca.1746–1748) shifts the positions of the buildings to allow a view down the Via del Quirinale.

PALAZZO DELLA CONSULTA, QUIRINALE

The palazzo is on the southeast corner of the Piazza del Quirinale. The facade was designed in 1732 for Clement XII by the leading architect of the time, Ferdinando Fuga. The design is similar to Bernini's Palazzo Chigi-Odescalchi (p. 182). The Consulta had broad judicial and administrative powers, and the building housed both cardinals and cavalry. It is now the seat of the Constitutional Court. Piranesi's engraving (ca. 1757–1758) rearranges the space to bring the Palazzo del Quirinale (p. 175) closer to the Consulta and to provide a view down Via del Quirinale that is not possible from this vantage point.

CASA DEI CRESCENZI

In the twelfth century the powerful Crescenzi family built this tower as a fortress to defend the Aemelian Bridge, from which it collected tolls. The tower is constructed of fragments of classical buildings and copies of others. Piranesi engraving, 1756.

PALAZZO DI ONORIO III (SAVELLI)

The Savelli family ruled the access roads to the Tiber. Honorious III and Honorius IV, both of this family, tried to repopulate the Aventine Hill. Fragments and the wall of their thirteenth-century stronghold remain on the summit of this hill. The fortress was destroyed by fire in 1313 by order of Emperor Henry VII.

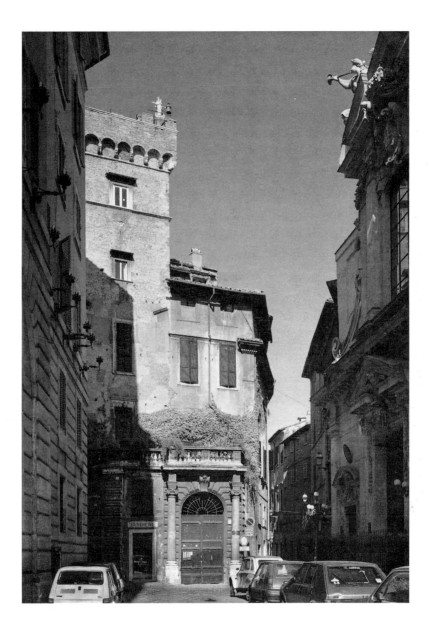

TORRE DELLA SCIMMIA

This thirteenth-century tower was built by the Crescenzi family to defend their neighboring house. Legend tells of a monkey (*scimmia*) that snatched a baby from its mother's arms and carried it to the roof of the tower. When the baby was safely returned, the parents placed on the roof a shrine to the Virgin with an "everlasting light." In Hawthorne's *The Marble Faun*, one of his protagonists, the American artist Hilda, lives in the tower's dovecote.

PALAZZO FARNESE

In 1515, the powerful Cardinal Alessandro Farnese (who became Paul III in 1534) began work on this greatest of Roman Renaissance palaces. He gave the commission to his favorite architect, Antonio da Sangallo the Younger. When Sangallo died in 1546, Michelangelo took over the work. He added the upper story, the cornice, the frieze with the Farnese Lilies, and the window over the entrance. The Palazzo Farnese is now the home of the French Embassy. In the Piazza Farnese are two fountains created from Egyptian granite baths brought from the Baths of Caracalla in the sixteenth century. To the right, at the terminus of the Via dei Farnesi on the Via Giulia (p. 181), is the church of S. Maria della Morte designed by Fuga. Piranesi engraving, 1773.

VIA GIULIA

The 1-km long Via Giulia was planned by Julius II (1503–1513). It is still considered one of the world's great streets. On the left of this view, looking southeast, is the Palazzo Farnese (p. 180). Michelangelo designed a bridge to connect the Palazzo Farnese to the Farnesina across the Tiber, which was never built. This arch connects the Palazzo Farnese with S. Maria della Morte.

PALAZZO CHIGI-ODESCALCHI

On the west (left) side of the narrow Piazza dei SS. Apostoli is the Palazzo Chigi-Odescalchi. The facade was designed by Bernini in 1664. The palazzo was purchased by the Odescalchi family in 1746. They had architects Nicola Salvi and Luigi Vanvitelli alter it significantly, doubling its length. To the east of the piazza is the Palazzo Colonna and the church of SS. Apostoli. In the Piranesi engraving (ca. 1757–1758) he "pushed" the Palazzo Colonna further to the north so that more of it would be visible.

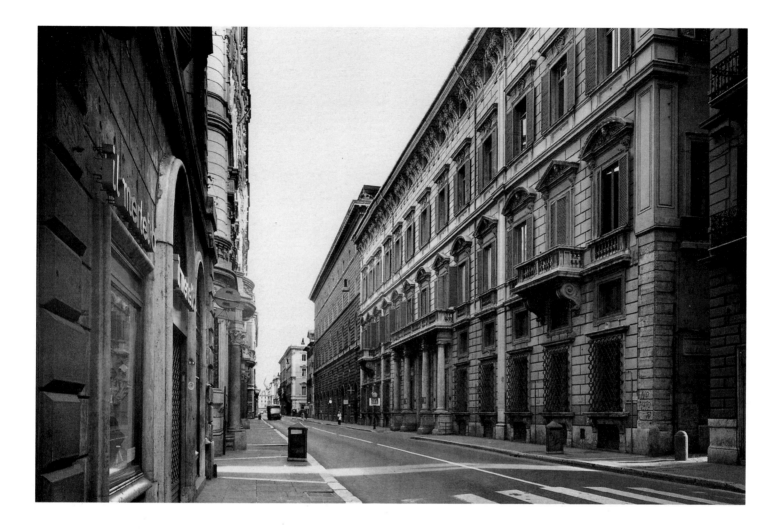

PALAZZO SALVIATI

Owned by the Salviati family in 1533, the palazzo was renovated in 1660 by Rainaldi, and further enlarged by Tommaso de' Marchis in the eighteenth century. During the eighteenth century, it served as the home of the French Academy in Rome (now located in the Villa Medici). This 6 A.M. view depicts unusual tranquillity on one of Rome's busiest avenues. Piranesi engraving, ca. 1757.

VILLA AURELIA

The Villa Aurelia was built in the mid-seventeenth century by the Farnese family and later became the home of Count Savorelli. Garibaldi established his headquarters here in 1849, and the French, in turn, bombarded the villa. The City of Rome later restored it. In 1881 the villa was purchased by the American heiress Mrs. Clara Jessup Heyland, who willed it to the American Academy in Rome. This view was taken from the photographer's studio at the American Academy.

VILLA PAMPHILJ

The villa and its gardens were praised by Goethe and painted by Corot. Now public, it is the largest park in Rome. The villa was designed in 1650 by Alessandro Algardi for Prince Camillo, nephew of Innocent X. The cubical country house, the Casino della Statue, was built between 1645 and 1647 and was originally designed with wings on either side. The 1776 Piranesi engraving exaggerates the effect of the garden's three descending terraces.

1850–1900

1900–1920

MODERN ERA

FORO ITALICO

E. U. R.

PIAZZA MONTAIGNE, E. U. R.

MODERN ROME

UFFICIO GEOLOGICA

The Ufficio Geologica (now a museum of agriculture) was founded in Florence in 1869. Its offices were transferred to Rome in 1873. In this 1873 building Raffaele Cabevari used steel beams, cast-iron columns, and exposed bolts for both their decorative and functional value. It is located near the Fontana dell'Acqua Felice.

PIAZZA COLONNA

The Piazza Colonna was the center of Roman activity for centuries. The base of the column of Marcus Aurelius is seen on the right. The Palazzo Wedekind, built in 1838, is the present home of the newspaper *Il Tempo*. It has 12 marble columns brought from the town of Vieo. Rossini engraving, ca. 1836.

ST. PAUL'S EPISCOPAL

This neo-Gothic Episcopal church, located on the corner of Via Nazionale and Via Napoli, was designed by George E. Street in 1879 and contains a mosaic by the British Pre-Raphaelite painter and muralist Sir Edward Burne-Jones.

CAMPO VERANO CIMITERO

The municipal cemetery was built on the grounds of the estate of Emperor Lucius Verus
(161–169). The entrance was designed by Virginio Vespignani between 1874 and 1878. The four
large allegorical figures represent Silence, Charity, Hope, and Meditation.

PALAZZO DELL'ESPOSIZIONE

The neoclassical palazzo was designed by Pio Piacentini and completed in 1882. It is located on
the Via Nazionale and is one of the major exhibition centers in Rome.

ACCADEMIA AMERICANA A ROMA

In 1883, a group of architects and artists, including Charles F. McKim and Augustus Saint-Gaudens, sought to create a permanent American institution in Rome. With the financial assistance of Carnegie, Rockefeller, Vanderbilt, and Frick, the American School of Architecture in Rome was established in 1884. It was chartered in 1905 as the American Academy in Rome. It is one of the foremost centers in the world for the practice of the fine arts and advanced research in the humanities. Designed by McKim, Mead & White, the building was completed in 1914.

PALAZZO DI GIUSTIZIA

Next to the Castel S. Angelo is the ornate Palace of Justice, designed by Giulielmo Calderini and built between 1880 and 1911. It was constructed of solid travertine and has sculptures by Ximenes and Quattrini. In 1970 the palazzo was in danger of collapse. It is so generally disliked that it is often called *Il Palazzaccio*, <u>the</u> ugly palazzo. St. Peter's can be seen beneath the bridge.

194

S. GIOACCHINO

S. Gioacchino is located west of Piazza del Popolo, across the Tiber on Via Pompeo Magno. Built by Raffaele Inganni in 1890, it commemorates the sacerdotal jubilee of Pope Leo XIII (Gioacchino Pecci).

CASA APARTAMENTE, VIA ARENULA

This large apartment building was built in 1895 by Camillo Boggio and Giulio Podesti. Its design
is characteristic of the eclectic styles of the late nineteenth century that borrowed from the neoclassical, baroque, and Renaissance.

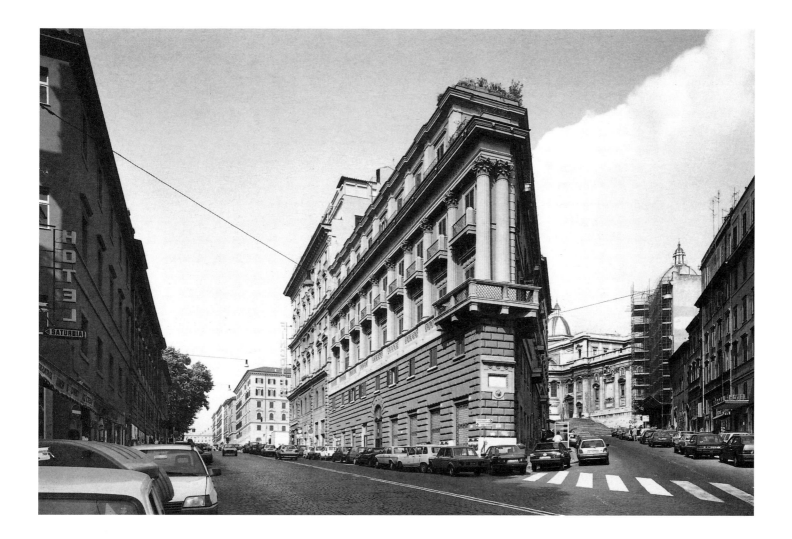

PALAZZO GIORGIOLI, VIA CAVOUR

Carlo Busiri Vici designed this apartment building on the Via Cavour in 1886. S. Maria Maggiore
is visible at the end of the street to the right.

ALBERGO SELECT, "IL MESSAGGERO"

Arturo Dazzi designed the Albergo (Hotel) Select in 1910. Like many other buildings of this era,
it borrows from fin de siècle French architecture. It is now used as an office building for the daily
newspaper *Il Messaggero*.

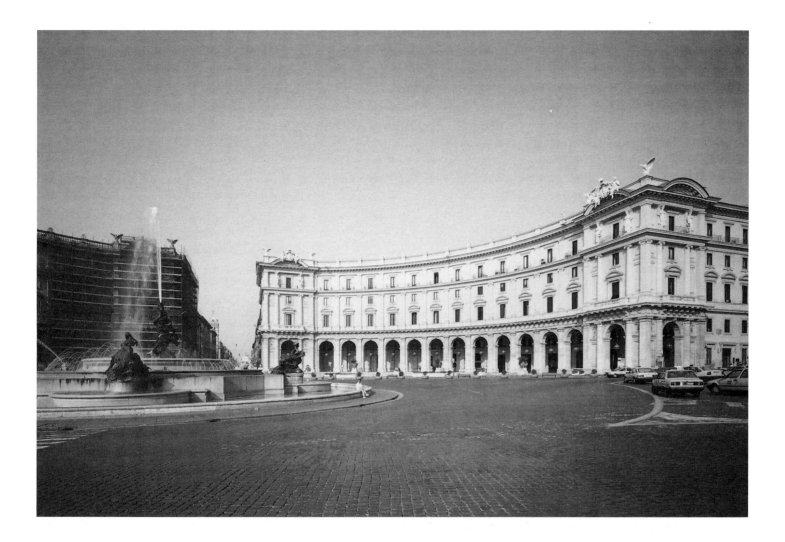

EDIFICI DELL'ESEDRA

The Piazza della Repubblica (also called the Piazza dell'Esedra) is an excellent example of post-1870 Roman town planning. The Edifici dell'Esedra, two large buildings designed by Gaetano Koch in 1896, define the southwest quadrant of the piazza and trace the curved southwest wall (the exedra) of the Baths of Diocletian (pp. 142, 144). The style of the porticoes reflects the architecture of Turin, home of Vittorio Emanuele II, king of the United Kingdom of Italy. The Naiad Fountain was built in 1885.

PALAZZO DELLE BELLE ARTI

The museum was designed by Cesare Bazzani in 1911 and enlarged in 1933. It contains the collection of the National Gallery of Modern Art, founded in 1883.

ACCADEMIA BRITANNICA A ROMA

The British Academy was first established as a School of Archaeology in 1901. The Commune di Roma offered the site to the school in 1912, following the International Exhibition of Fine Arts in Rome the year before. Sir Edwin Lutyens designed the west facade, based upon the west facade of St. Paul's Cathedral. In the surrounding Viale delle Belle Arti region are academies from Belgium, Holland, Sweden, Romania, and Austria.

MONUMENTO A VITTORIO EMANUELE II

"Il Vittoriano" was designed by Giuseppi Sacconi in 1855 and inaugurated in 1911 to symbolize King Vittorio Emanuele II's unification of Italy. From its inception, its design has drawn heated controversy and scorn. More than 80 meters high, it is built of a bright white marble incongruous with Rome's warm brick. Its overwhelming scale has forever changed the Roman skyline. It houses the grave of Italy's Unknown Soldier from World War I. In the foreground are columns from the Forum of Trajan.

PONTE DEL RISORGIMENTO

Begun in 1909 and inaugurated in 1911, this 100-meter long single-span bridge connects the Piazza Monte Grappa with the Piazzale delle Belle Arti. Designed by the engineer Francois Hennebique, it was the first reinforced-concrete bridge built in Rome.

MINISTERO DELLA PUBBLICA ISTRUZIONE

This excessively ornate building on the Viale Trastevere was designed by Cesare Bazzani in 1920.
It was against this type of architecture that the futurists and rationalists fought.

LA RINASCENTE

Designed in 1860 by Giulio de Angelis, La Rinascente was first called the Palazzo dei Grande Magazzini (department store) Bocconi. Although modern in its use of glass and steel, its multistoried arcades recall earlier Roman architectural traditions.

GALLERIA COLONNA

The Galleria Colonna is located on the east side of the Piazza Colonna (also p. 189), across the Via Corso. It was designed in 1914 by Dario Carbone for the Banca Italiana di Sconto. Built on the site of the demolished Palazzo Piombino, it has an interior arcade, shops, and cafès.

MINISTERO DELLA MARINA

Located on the east bank of the Tiber by the Ponte Matteotti, the Ministry of the Marine was
designed by Giulio Magni in 1928.

SCUOLA E. BATTISTI, GARBATELLA

The planners of Garbatella specifically wanted to avoid the monotony they saw in other European garden suburbs. In contrast, they sought to design picturesque streets and vistas, placing important buildings on main street axes. This school was designed in 1930 by Brunetto. Like many buildings from this era, it was allowed to deteriorate almost irreparably. It is now being restored.

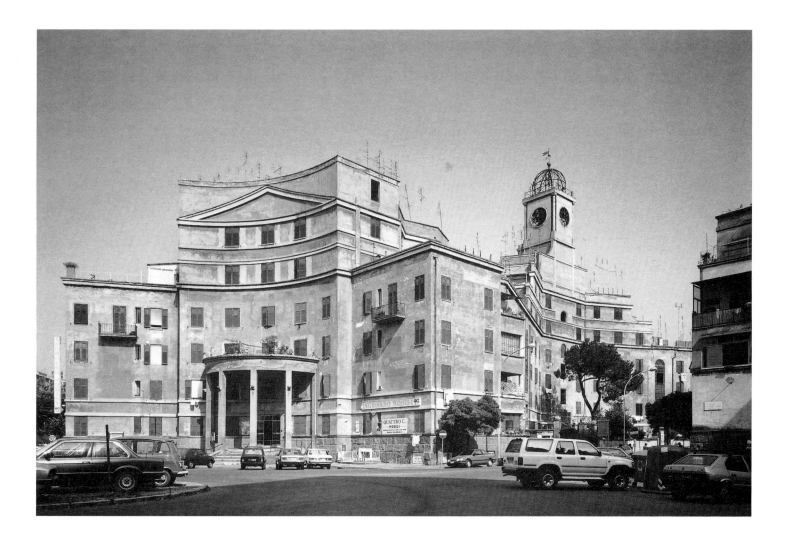

ALBERGO SUBURBANO, GARBATELLA

Innocenzo Sabbatini joined the new Institute for Public Housing in 1919. Though not a strict rationalist, Sabbatini joined the group, seeking new solutions to public housing for the rapidly expanding population. His four housing blocks for the new garden suburb of Garbatella, built in 1927, departed from the Italian tradition of large structures built around open-air courtyards. His buildings were often characterized by wings radiating from a central block. Some even included communal dining facilities.

PIAZZA SEMPIONE, ANIENE

This garden-city region of Monte Sacro near the River Aniene was planned in 1920 by Gustavo
Giovannoni. The central building, with its rustic and medieval allusions, was designed by
Innocenzo Sabbatini.

CASA MADRE DEI MUTILATI

Built between 1928 and 1937 by Marcello Piacentini, the building is located just east of Castel S. Angelo. Son of the well-known Roman architect, Pio Piacentini, Marcello became one of the leading architects of this period. He considered the aesthetic foundations of architecture superior to its more technical considerations and questioned the appropriateness of the rationalists' unadorned architecture.

211

PALAZZO POSTALE, VIA MARMORATA

The National Ministry of Transportation and Communication held a competition for the design of four post offices in Rome. In 1933 Adalberto Libera, one of the leaders of the rationalist movement, was awarded the commission for this site on the Aventine close to the Pyramid of Caius Cestius. The large and as-then-unbuilt site allowed Libera, together with Mario De Renzi, to design a modern monument surrounded by generous landscape. The building has a colonnade, a public hall, and a U-shaped office block.

STAZIONE TERMINI

Trains first entered Rome in about 1856 with only three lines serving the city. In 1938, plans began for the new Stazione Termini, so named for its proximity to the Baths (Terme) of Diocletian. The war halted its construction in 1942. The station was finally finished in 1950 and is one of the largest in Europe. This view shows the northwest entrance with its dramatic cantilevered portico.

PIAZZALE FORO ITALICO

The Foro Italico, a sports center, was built in 1931 and was the site of the 1960 Olympics. The Fontana della Sfera, in the foreground, was designed in 1930 by Mario Paniconi and Giulio Pediconi. In the distance is the 17-meter monolith inscribed "Mussolini Dux," designed in 1932 by Constantino Constantini.

ACCADEMIA DI EDUCAZIONE FISICA, FORO ITALICO

Renato Ricci, the zealous director of the organization charged with the physical development of Italian youth, selected Enrico Del Debbio to design the Foro Mussolini, now called the Foro Italico. For his 1922 design, Del Debbio combined strong geometric elements with aspects of the Milanese-based decorative novocento (1900s) style, such as the details around the windows. Designers of the novocento movement represented many design philosophies, but were united in a desire to develop a "new" architecture for Italy.

STADIO DEI MARMI, FORO ITALICO

Del Debbio designed the vast Stadio dei Marmi in 1928 as part of the Foro Italico. The stadium holds 20,000 spectators and features 60 monumental statues of athletes.

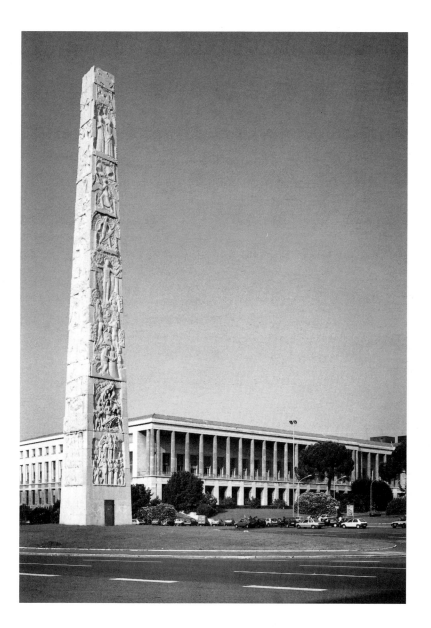

PIAZZA MARCONI, E.U.R.

Marcello Piacentini began plans for the grandly ambitious Esposizione Universale di Roma (E.U.R.) in 1938. Scheduled to open in 1942, it was designed to symbolize the achievements of fascism and link Rome and Ostia along the new motorway. E.U.R. and the Foro Italico are the best examples of Roman neoimperial city planning. War halted construction in 1941; it was resumed in 1951. The 45-meter Carrara marble stela was designed by Arturo Dazzi.

MUSEO DI CIVILTÀ ROMANA, E.U.R.

Financed by FIAT, this museum was designed between 1939 and 1941 by Pietro Aschieri, D. Bernardini, and Cesare Pascoletti. It contains 59 rooms with displays illustrating the history and influence of Rome, and a room-sized scale model of fourth-century Rome. Aschieri was one of the earliest outspoken members of the Italian rationalist architecture movement.

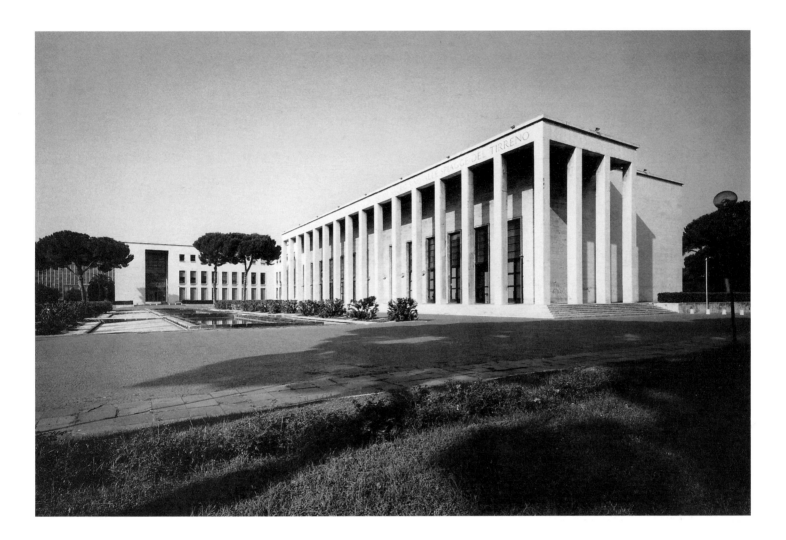

PALAZZO DEGLI UFICCI, E. U. R.

This striking example of rationalist architecture was designed by Gaetano Minnucci in 1937.
Together with Adalberto Libera, Minnucci organized the first exhibition of rationalist architecture
and was among its most articulate spokesmen.

PALAZZI INA E INPS, E.U.R.

Giovanni Muzio, a proponent of the novocento style, was considered the preeminent architect of the 1920s. His desire for a modern interpretation of neoclassical style is evident in his design for what was then called the Porta Imperiale. The exedra (one of two facing each other across the Via Cristoforo) has beautifully spaced and elegantly proportioned columns.

PALAZZO DEI RICEVIMENTI E CONGRESSI, E.U.R.

Adalberto Libera was one of the principal figures in the Italian rationalist architecture movement and his built projects are among the very best of the era (see also p. 212). In 1938, Libera won the competition for this key building in the E.U.R. complex. His design included a square reception hall covered by a monumental cross vault and an open-air theater on the roof.

PALAZZO DELLA CIVILTÀ ITALICA, E. U. R.

Designed in 1939 by Giovanni Guerrini, Ernesto La Padula, and Mario Romano, the Palazzo della
Civiltà Italica is also known as the Palazzo della Civiltà del Lavoro and the Square Colosseum.
Standing on the highest point in E.U.R., the palazzo is 70 meters high, with 216 arches on 6
floors. The arches symbolize the heritage of Roman architecture; their repetition represents the
endurance of Roman civilization. The design generated criticism that continues to this day.

SS. PIETRO E PAOLO, E.U.R.

SS. Pietro e Paolo, built between 1931 and 1941, marks the terminus of Viale Europa. Designed by
Arnoldo Foschini, its dome is almost as large as that of St. Peter's. The bronze doors, with low
reliefs illustrating the lives of Saints Peter and Paul, were designed by Giovanni Prini.

INDEX